FIRST AID IN
COUNSELLING

FIRST AID IN COUNSELLING

Editor

C. L. MITTON

EDINBURGH: T. & T. CLARK, 38 GEORGE STREET

PRINTED IN ENGLAND BY
THE SCOLAR PRESS LIMITED
FOR
T. & T. CLARK LTD., EDINBURGH

0 567 22304 3

First printed . . . 1968
Latest impression . . 1977

CONTENTS

Preface vii

1 PROBLEMS OF ADOLESCENCE. By Michael
   Hare Duke 9

2 THE SIXTH FORM AGNOSTIC. By H. G.
   Dickinson 21

3 THE DELINQUENT IN TROUBLE WITH THE
   LAW—AND HIS WORRIED PARENTS.
   By William L. Carrington . . . 29

4 THE PREGNANT SINGLE GIRL AND HER
   PARENTS. By Kenneth G. Greet . 40

5 WHERE A MARRIAGE BREAKDOWN IS
   THREATENED. By William L. Carrington 51

6 THE MOTHER WHOSE CHILDREN ARE NOW
   GROWN UP AND NO LONGER NEED HER
   AS ONCE THEY DID. By William L.
   Carrington 63

7 THE DESERTED WIFE, HUSBAND, OR
   CHILDREN. By William L. Carrington 74

8 THE CARE OF THE AGED. By Anthony
   Bashford 86

9 CHRISTIAN MINISTRY TO THE DYING. By
   Sydney Evans 98

10 THE BEREAVED. By William L. Carrington 107

11 MEN UNDER ATTACK. By Michael Hare
   Duke 118

12 THE THREATENED NERVOUS BREAK-
   DOWN : PART 1. By Frank Lake . 126

13 THE THREATENED NERVOUS BREAK-
DOWN : PART 2. By Frank Lake   .   138

14 THE SUICIDAL EMERGENCY. By Howard
J. Clinebell   148

15 THE CLERGYMAN'S RÔLE IN THE ALCO-
HOLIC EMERGENCY. By Howard J.
Clinebell   160

16 DRUG ADDICTION. By Norman W.
Imlah   173

17. THE HOMOSEXUAL MAN. By Frank
Lake   183

18 THE CHURCH AND THE IMMIGRANT. By
T. Geoffrey Ayre   196

19 UPROOTED PEOPLE. By Norman S.
Power   206

20 COMMUNITY AND COMMUNICATION. By
Brian Lake   214

PREFACE

EARLY in 1965 as editor of THE EXPOSITORY
TIMES I wrote to a small but representative group
of our regular readers asking their advice. I put
before them a number of subjects on which a
series of articles could be commissioned, and
asked them to arrange them in order of preference.
The one which came first was entitled ' First Aid
in Counselling '. This was no surprise, since to-day
this is the area in which most ministers long to be
experts, and yet often find themselves ill-equipped.
We think we ought to know how to help people out
of their distresses and disablements into a really
full and worth-while life, and yet sometimes we
feel very inadequate, if not quite helpless.

It was with the hope of providing needed
guidance in this important area of pastoral
responsibility that we enlisted the help of numerous
experts, not only from Great Britain, but also from
Australia and the U.S.A., not only from the
ordained ministry but also from the ranks of
doctors and social workers. Each one was asked
from their own area of specialized skill to write an
article to help the non-specialist to deal wisely
with those who came with one or other of the
many recurring types of human need. These
articles appeared in THE EXPOSITORY TIMES
between November 1965 and September 1967.

The series was called ' *First Aid* in Counselling '.
This was partly because we recognized that in a
short article a full treatment of a difficult situation
was not possible. It was also partly because
certain serious cases may have to be referred, after
some preliminary inquiries, either to some trained
expert such as a psychiatrist, or to some specialized
group whose sole purpose is to help those in
special kinds of distress, e.g., the alcoholic or the
suicidal. In other cases the minister or pastoral

worker may well have to provide the entire treatment. In these instances the articles aim to tell us how to make the right start and how to proceed along the right lines.

The series has clearly met a real need and has been widely appreciated. For this reason it now appears in book form, to be available conveniently to those who already know the separate articles, and also to reach to a wider public. We hope that it will be a means of strengthening the pastoral work of many ministries.

C. L. MITTON

I. Problems of Adolescence

By the Reverend Michael Hare Duke,
The Clinical Theology Centre, Nottingham

' Would there were no age between ten and three-and-twenty, or that youth would sleep out the rest; for there is nothing in-between, but getting wenches with child, wronging the ancientry, stealing, fighting.'

So the Shepherd complains in ' The Winter's Tale '. It is as good a text as any for reminding ourselves that the transition from childhood to adult life tends always to be a difficult one in any generation.

The New Testament also seems to expect that there will be a conflict. The pull of parental authority may hinder a man from finding his true identity in the service of God. So we find Jesus saying :

If anyone come to me and does not hate his father and mother, wife and children, brothers and sisters, even his own life, he cannot be a disciple of mine.

There is also the incident reported of His attitude to parental duty in Luke 9[59-62] :

To another he said, ' Follow me ', but the man replied, ' Let me go and bury my father first '. Jesus said, ' Leave the dead to bury their dead ; you must go and announce the Kingdom of God '.

Yet another said, ' I will follow you, sir ; but let me first say good-bye to my people at home '. To him Jesus said, ' No one who sets his hand to the plough and then keeps looking back is fit for the Kingdom of God '.

This may at first appear a different problem from the complaint of our opening quotation. In fact they would seem to be different aspects of a similar situation which may in general be called the ' crisis of identity ' in adolescence. In leaving his parents' control the child is trying to become a person in his own right. To do this he may find himself driven to violent expressions of rebellion. His methods may be socially unacceptable but at

9

least he has a theological sanction for seeking in some way to break free to a life of his own.

The problems which then emerge can be subsumed under the three main headings of *Personal Relationships*, *Authority* and *Work*. First of all that of personal relationships. Here the awareness of sexuality in a new form at puberty is the most powerful new factor. There is all the excitement and sense of discovery in the new physical sensations and emotional drives. Alongside this, however, society tends to build-in some stringent prohibitions backed by the threat of a condemnation. The young person is faced with the question, ' What do I do with my new awareness ?' This can be answered at the physical level in terms of masturbation or sexual experiment, or chastity. But this is only part of the problem, though very often the young feel that it is the one upon which the adult world most concentrates. For them there is the much deeper question of discovering whether one is acceptable to the opposite sex, and if one fears that one is not, facing very early the terror of loneliness.

In a discussion with a group of young people on the topic of *personal relationships*, it emerged from both boys and girls that their first emotion in a dance-hall was one of inadequacy. The boys admitted that they stayed in a bunch on the edge of the floor, largely for fear that if one of them detached himself from the group and asked a girl to dance he might get turned down. The girls, on the other hand, admitted that when approached by a boy they were afraid that they would not match up to his expectations. They took the easier way out of getting on to the floor by dancing with a girl-friend ! It seems that all young people, as they advance into adulthood, have to ask themselves the question whether their manhood or their womanhood is really an adequate one, whether they can fulfil the rôle which is biologically thrust upon them.

The next series of questions facing the teenager may be characterized under the word *authority*. This is the challenge of the move from the dependent rôle of the child to that of the responsible adult. It involves questioning many of the pre-suppositions on which one has been brought up, not necessarily in order to reject them, but to make them one's own. Such questioning, however, can frequently lead to conflict with parents who are not ready to relinquish their hold over a child. ' My mum's always fussing over my hair. " Get your hair cut," she says. " Why don't you look a proper man ",' was a typical comment on the problems of parents by an eighteen-year-old member of a Youth Club. He was allowed to drive the family car, but mother still could not relinquish her right to pat his hair into place and tell him when to go to the barber. The essential conflict with authority seems to develop at home but it has its ramifications both in behaviour at school and in the rejection of codes of behaviour or forms of belief which seem to have an authoritarian background.

Finally there is the move-out into the world of *work*. When he leaves school and takes on his first job, the young person has got to take his own decisions about what he hopes from life in terms of ambition. He must also learn to handle his own money and decide what his aims are, whether of enjoyment, saving for security or payment to the home finances.

In all these areas of his life the pressure is to-wards adulthood and independence. There is a large part of any personality which is ready to move forward. On the other hand each of these res-ponsibilities requires a great deal of courage. In all three spheres the child is becoming the man and having to take a decision to stand alone. There is always bound to be a regretful, backward glance to the security when others took the decisions for him and, therefore, also took the blame if anything went wrong. At this age the young person tends to want to have it both ways, to have the right to choose for himself and not to relinquish the privilege of his parents' protection. Indeed he even goes so far as to project on to them his accusation of unfairness against the tensions in which he finds himself by the very fact of adolescence.

This situation would be enough to create its

difficulties were it without further complications. Unfortunately we are none of us endowed with ideal parents and they do not necessarily react with understanding or maturity to these difficult times. Perhaps the commonest reaction is one of bewilderment : ' He never used to be like that ', says many a perplexed father or mother. So they look round for explanations. There are always plenty of scapegoats to hand. The blame can be put on the television, saying it gives young people such a bad example. We can say that the schools are at fault : ' They don't teach them any discipline nowadays ', is the cry. Or we can look round and decide that our children were led into bad habits by the example of their friends. There may be some truth in all these explanations, but yet if we leave things there, it seems that the great opportunity of adolescence will be missed and we shall be left thinking of this new stage in our children's life simply as ' a problem time ' that has got to be struggled through.

It is, however, a time with creative possibilities repeating some of the opportunities of the first years of infancy. It is interesting to notice how, even in the language we use about the two stages, there seems to be much similarity. Once we watched our son staggering from chair to chair keeping his balance. Now we say that he must learn to stand on his own feet. In infancy we listened to his first syllables lisped out ; now we hear him learning to talk the language of the world. Instead of the supplies that mother once provided, now we talk of him earning his bread and butter. In this perhaps there is a clue as to what is going on. We are going again over the old ground, facing the crises of living in a new mode.

How the adolescent responds to this challenge of development will very much depend upon how the initial crises were handled in infancy. If his early days were an experience of tolerance and understanding then this will be the child's image of the universe. This will be what he naturally expects from the adult world and indeed from God Himself. There will be some confidence that, as he moves out to attempt the new feats of development, the same good-will will sustain him. If, before, he found who he was by the friendly response of the world around him, he has no cause to doubt that he will find himself again with a new identity as an adult man.

But suppose this were not the case. Suppose instead that he looked out from that extraordinarily observant watch-post that is manned in the family by the infant and saw not tranquillity, but anxiety. He may have seen the parents uncertain about their own relationship one to another; when he looked for a pattern of manhood in his father, he may have found a weak person, pushed to the periphery of family life, dancing attendance upon the mother, who gave him orders and ruled the home. He has no choice but to absorb the pattern even though another part of him rejects it fiercely. When later he comes to expect a relationship with a woman himself, there are going to be special anxieties built-in to the experiment for him. Though sixteen years have passed still his father will be there. He may feel a desire to turn to him for advice and help ; he will also want to accuse him of the failure to give him the pattern of manhood that he could have made his own. Father, meekly sitting on the touch-line still, will find it hard to understand what it is his son is resenting.

Or perhaps it is not so much the anxieties which a child observes sparking between his parents ; it may be that he himself is the stimulus for reminding them of their own hidden needs. A father with unconscious memories of his own childhood will be conditioned towards his baby.

A father reported that at one time one of his children reverted to bed-wetting under emotional stress. Although he could accept this rationally, yet he found himself having to restrain an intense fury with the child when he actually was in the room dealing with the wet sheets. His own mother had always said what an ideal baby he had been, dry by the age of six months !

What will the effect of this be ? In such cases the children will learn, perhaps, to respond to their father's anger and pattern their habits acceptably for him. Later, they must face the question of how they order the rest of their lives and still the dominating father will be there to urge them to keep their accounts, to fold their clothes, to stack their books away. Somewhere the pattern of his compulsive authority will either have to be challenged in the conscious world or they will knuckle under and repress their apparently unacceptable side.

Or again the baby may be aware of the hopeless inconsistency of emotional response that it finds in the adult world. Sometimes there is pleasure and delight in what it does ; sometimes the same action is met with punishment and rebuke. This is typically the case with a mother who, from her own immaturity, can sometimes tolerate the natural joy and exuberance of her children, sometimes has to quell it almost punitively as she feels it threatens and exhausts her, perhaps bringing on her regular migraine. From such treatment children can come to believe that life is a battle in which you cannot win.

Here one can see the seeds of the adolescent conflict being sown. The tragedy is that parents who have no chance to gain insight are caught in the trap of compulsive repetition. To the outside observer or the case-worker hearing the story afterwards, there seems to be a tragic inevitability in the repetition of the mistakes. This is perhaps the first thing that the Church needs to say about adolescence, that it is an opportunity for repentance and a new start. All of us do damage to our children, for, as parents, we none of us are free from the hidden needs which drive our conduct against all reason. But if in the years in which our children grow up beside us we are prepared to let them be the mirror in which we look for the insight into our own inadequacies, they have much to teach us. By the time they have reached adolescence there is a real chance that we can go over the problems of infancy, but this time get them right.

Imagine a father who, with the arrival of his first child, found himself bitterly jealous and responding to this either by a terrible strictness or else by absenting himself as much as he could from the house. Over the years, his child will have told him, first in infant language, that he is a ' horrid daddy ', or will have pleaded for more of his time. Later the same insight will have been offered, perhaps not in words but in behaviour. It is tragic if the parent still needs to defend his ideal image of himself against his child and cannot respond with humility and repentance to the appeal for love. Yet such an act requires a new security to be given to the parent. Left to ourselves we hide away from the accusation that our children make against us. One has found a number of instances in professional people who had a high degree of insight into the problem of others, yet have consistently refused to recognize the level of disturbed behaviour in their own children.

Mr. D., a caseworker, had an adopted son of ten. There were no children of his own. At about the age of two the child had shown symptoms of disturbance and had been admitted to a paediatric unit for investigation. Neurological and other physical tests proved negative. Mr. D. does not seem to have made any further enquiries concerning the possibilities of emotional disturbance. The child has had a history of unhappy school relationships. The local school asked for his removal and he was sent to a boarding school from which anxious enquiries are now being sent to his parents. The local clergyman was consulted as the mother expressed her belief that some religious instruction might help the boy and also wondered whether he might respond to the laying on of hands.

In consultation with a priest the mother admitted that she felt a great deal of guilt towards the child. When he first arrived she feels that she consciously ' held back from him '. She explains this by saying that she had often heard that when you have a baby in the house a woman who has previously been sterile may conceive. She desperately wanted a baby of her own and was determined that if she did become pregnant before the adoption formalities were completed she would return the child. In the course of further conversation it became clear that both parents felt deeply ashamed that their child should have difficulties. For a long period the father said that he had tried the

15

severest measures of physical punishment to control the child, especially his aggressive behaviour towards the mother.

The consultation which opened up these topics ended with the suggestion that a psychiatric assessment of the child was indicated. A subsequent letter reported that the parents had decided instead to ask for further physical investigations.

Another instance of parental guilt was to be observed in the case of a young woman in her early twenties suffering from a psychotic illness. Her disturbance seemed to provoke her parents into a punitive threat of ' shutting her up ' in a mental hospital. One had the feeling that one was intruding upon a much earlier scene where the parents must have said, ' If you speak to us like that again, you'll go to bed '.

In all this then is a double work for the Church. First of all the helping of Christian parents to an insight into what is happening in the family relationships, but secondly and much more importantly giving the motive for the restoring of relationships. ' To us is committed the ministry of reconciliation.' We tend to think of this commission in terms of reconciling conscious sinners into the community of the Church. The healed relationships in Christ ought to make the exchange of forgiveness of far wider relevance than that. Where ought we to start more importantly than within the family itself ?

As the young person sets out from home into the world of work he carries with him the attitudes towards authority which he learned in childhood. Anyone who is put in authority over him is going, at first, to be met as though he were wearing a mask of ' father ', whether this be good or bad, and only when experience has proved otherwise, will he be able to come clear and be known in his own right. In addition, however, the boy or girl is having to find his own place in society. He is now treated as part of the grown-up world, and, according to the level of his anxiety about his status as a person, he will try to conform to what is expected of him or strike out in a line of his own.

He may already have found a double standard

in his world of values between school and home. At the latter father comes back from work, having ' won ' some of his employer's property ; he may not have a high standard of integrity in matters of time and work done, or of loyalty to his employer. At school all these qualities will have been greatly stressed. The boy or girl may, therefore, feel himself torn between what he knows is inculcated at school and what he sees in his parents. It is likely, however, that even the most cynical of parents will have shielded their children from some of the cold blasts of actual industrial practice. The school leaver has, therefore, got to adjust himself to the behaviour of the group he works with, both in matters of honesty, sexual morality and personal integrity. Such a situation makes for great difficulty. It takes courage to be one's self naturally and easily in such varying circumstances and the young person may very well find himself adopting various masks in order to be acceptable according to the place in which he is.

If the young person has not found satisfactory patterns for his life in mother and father he will be casting round for them elsewhere. Here is the second rôle of the Church. Its primary purpose is to create a Christian family where forgiveness and love prevail. If, however, that does not succeed it must think in terms of the substitute family. Perhaps we may even see the age-long practice of providing God-parents at the Christening as something of a safe-guard in just this direction.

The latter is no doubt highly desirable and might be considered as a possibility for the future. Meanwhile one must recognize that in hard practice the place, where most people actually turn to find someone who will take over the rôle of a father or mother who has failed, is in the two people with whom they come in contact in the form of the Parson and the Schoolteacher. This is not a matter of urging people to undertake a new rôle with perhaps some dangerous psychological overtones ; it is rather a realistic acceptance of what is already happening. It is all too easy for us to avoid admitting quite how important we are to many young people with whom we come in contact. It is almost as though we dared not undertake so great a burden of responsibility. Yet one is bound to recognize that the child whose parenting is inadequate will look round for a substitute to fill out his longing for an ideal father and his projections can easily be directed towards the Vicar, the Curate, or his Schoolteacher. In so far as a person is struggling with unsatisfied needs out of the past, their demands are likely to be of a kind which we can never hope to satisfy. If their actual father represents to them a sense of failure, they will be looking for an ideal father who never lets them down. When we find ourselves in this position it is dangerously easy to start by feeling flattered and try to live up to the ideals which are thrust upon us. If we do, we are bound to fail. What is required is that we should be sensitive to what the child is asking and by means of that awareness try to help him to a realistic understanding of the world in which all adults are both bad and good. If we can learn to understand and accept the good projections, perhaps it will also help us to tolerate the bad ones. For we help people not only by responding to their hope of goodness but also by allowing them to find a person on whom to focus their hostility, who does not kick back unreasonably or destroy them in the way that their neurotic self fears might be the case.

Our aim as Christians, however, is not merely to accept the human needs of those who come in contact with us as any effective and well-trained case-worker might, but rather to point people beyond ourselves to that which ultimately gives a meaning to the whole of life, the Person of God Himself. We cannot do this in a vacuum. It is as we prove trustworthy recipients of their varied emotions that they are able more easily to believe in the Faith which we can offer them. Yet in saying this, one is not urging anyone working with young people to import a doctrine which does not naturally spring out of the communication which is taking place between them already. It is the worker's genuine interest in the boy or girl and their world which is the vital contribution, not an artificially introduced ' God-language '. This is especially important when one remembers the situations out of the past which will condition a person's picture of God. We all begin by patterning Him on the image of our parents—mother as well as father. There is inherent in youth an idealistic, almost perfectionist side, which one knows responds to the stimulus of challenge. While this may properly be evoked by the ideals of the Christian faith, yet in some people this can lead to intolerable conflict. They feel that there is a demand from God that they should be the perfect offering. And yet with genuine self-knowledge they recognize that this is far from being the case with them. Therefore they are led to feel themselves guilty because of all their imperfections, or else to deny the imperfections at all and split off part of themselves. This is most likely to occur in the field of adolescent sexuality where masturbation will most certainly produce very deep guilt feelings in anyone whose patterning is this way. In the same ' all-or-nothing ' approach of youth there will be an appeal in any kind of religious affirmation which demands complete acceptance. This may be either of the fundamentalist or rigidly Catholic brand. The maturity of tolerated doubt is something that has to be learned painfully and, to young people, can look very like the double-think of humbug. It is a narrow path that the wise Pastor needs to tread between accepting the youthful certainty of young people and trading on it for his own purposes.

Once again it is perhaps in ourselves that we need to look for an adjustment to the problem rather than in the young people. If we feel either threatened by their exuberant affirmation or have a need to use them in order to bolster our uncertainties we will not be wise guides to them. We will be unable to detect the occasions when, under the guise of a very aggressive statement, they are actually asking a question. We will be led into conflict with them rather than into the rôle of shepherds who lead.

Almost all the problems of adolescents can be seen ultimately as a question about who one is. In trying to answer it many of them look for an affirmation of themselves in sexual experience. Others find that they are so unsure of their identity that they find themselves unable to make the usual relationships and either seek those which seem more secure amongst their own sex or else withdraw altogether into isolation. This may be the time when deeply stressed persons first show their inability to make a relationship which will grow. It is evinced by the young person who says that ' People bore me ', ' There's nothing in life that I find worth living for '. It is a time too when one hopes for confirmation of who one is, from one's peer group as well as from the adult world ; one is desperately looking for approval and fearful of condemnation. The trouble is that if one has already decided that condemnation is bound to be the outcome, then one tries to forestall it by being aggressive and non-conformist instead.

The Christian Church should be the place when men at every period in their life find their value affirmed. It is particularly important that young people on the threshold of maturity should find that they are taken seriously. They do not want a disproportionate amount of attention, for, although flattering at first, it does not ultimately help them to see how they fit into the pattern of the adult world. They do not want to be considered as a ' problem ', but are grateful to those who can understand what they are feeling about the transitional stage between childhood and adult life and can help them move through some of the conflicting moods that it entails. As they find people who can do this out of the security of their own God-based identity they are likely to turn to the Church as a source of maturity rather than reject it as part of the childhood authority from which they want to grow free.

II. The Sixth Form Agnostic

By the Reverend H. G. Dickinson,
Chaplain, Winchester College

Our Sixth Form[1] population is only a tiny proportion of our whole society, and yet it is an important
group because its members will in time qualify for
many of the influential posts in our incipient
meritocracy. In twenty years' time their attitudes
to the Christian religion will doubtless carry a
disproportionate weight in our society. We are
therefore justified in paying special attention to the
content of our dialogue with them and also to the
methods we use both in group discussion and in
individual counselling.

There are hundreds of men and women in the
teaching profession who have had far longer
experience of dealing with the problems of agnos-
ticism in this age group than the present writer ;
but it seems to be true that throughout the country
there has developed in very recent years a new
climate of opinion among students and Sixth
formers, which is facing those who are involved
with them with a new pattern of problems. It is
very doubtful whether there are any straight-
forward solutions, but at least an accurate analysis
of the nature of these problems is the first step
towards dealing with them constructively.

Sixth formers are intelligent adolescents, but
their adolescence has a greater influence on their
religious beliefs than their intelligence. It does
not appear that their emotional attitudes are
different from those of their less able contemporaries ; only they have better equipment for
rationalizing their attitudes. The articulate
intelligence of a Sixth former may easily lead one
to believe that he has a corresponding maturity.
In fact the opposite may well be the case ; the
highly intelligent are often less emotionally stable

[1] This is shorthand for the age-group 17–19 already
or likely to be involved in higher education.

and more insecure in their personal relationships than their contemporaries. They may nevertheless have learned to use the language of maturity with a facility which conceals from themselves and their listener the underdevelopment of their emotional lives. This was sharply illustrated for me by the Headmaster of a Secondary Modern School who came to talk to a group of University students. Compared to his own 15-year-old leavers he felt that they were hardly out of the egg when it came to understanding what makes people tick. An intelligent youth may be conversant with Freud and yet more unperceptive about his own personal and family relationships than many 15-year-old leavers.

It is very easy for those who have to act as counsellors to this group of young people to misjudge the level at which many of their statements about religion are made. The conversation may appear on the surface to be primarily intellectual, but if one listens closely to the tone of voice and to the feeling-content of the words used one may frequently detect an entirely different level of meaning. The process is not unlike that adopted by Kremlinologists, who can decipher the realities of a political struggle for power under the apparent abstractions of a discussion of Marxism in *Pravda*.

Such a parallel, if left unqualified, might give the impression of an extreme scepticism about the independence of the intellect in guiding or forming a man's attitudes. Most of those who have lived in academic societies would, however, agree that a certain scepticism is sometimes justified ; the intelligent man seems often to be distinguished from his less able neighbour only in his ability to produce more plausible reasons for his prejudices. Sixth formers are no less prone to this weakness than the rest of us, but the pattern of their emotional responses is less complex and more predictable than that of their hardened elders. While we recognize that there is a genuine intellectual content to the difficulties in belief felt by this age-group, we must also be sensitive to the fact that what may look at first sight a statement from the head may on closer listening turn out to be a disguised expression of the feeling of the heart.

Religious issues impinge on areas that are emotionally sensitive for most adolescents. Religion is about personal identity in a group and personal and group relationships ; as Michael Hare Duke has pointed out these are acutely painful areas of experience for most adolescents. For many young people Christian morality seems to be primarily aimed at the elimination of self and the rigid regulation of sex ; and the adolescent is only just beginning to identify himself and is fascinated and appalled by his new sexuality. As he struggles to win freedom for his own identity the adolescent reacts strongly against any form of authoritarianism, and authority is often not distinguishable from authoritarianism. In most schools religion is inextricably entangled with ' the authorities ', and attitudes to the latter are soon transferred to the former, even if Christianity has not already been presented to the young as an authoritarian system. Adolescents to-day are particularly hostile to ' systems ' because they feel that their independence of thought and action, even their personal identity, is threatened by anything that looks like a strait-jacket of belief or precept which limits their own freedom to experiment. This may produce the odd, but quite common, phenomenon of an intelligent boy who is determinedly irrationalist in matters of religion. ' Religion is a private affair—everybody has to decide for himself what his religion is going to be.' There may even be hostility towards an intellectually rigorous and analytical approach to Christian evidences. This may possibly be due to a fear that the authority of disciplined inquiry is a threat to liberty of belief, or possibly it may be the same fear of ' taking things to pieces ' which is reflected in the common dislike of any close analysis of a work of literature.

This feeling that religion is essentially a subjective, intuitive, and private emotional experience is very deep-seated. Many adolescents who reject Christianity cling obstinately to the belief that

23

God is different for everyone; they find no difficulty in the supposition that two men may properly hold two radically inconsistent ideas about God, which cannot be logically reconciled. They resent the suggestion that one may be ' right ' and the other ' wrong ' in any but a conventional sense. Similarly they do not like to think that there might be an objective morality. ' It just happens that we have been conditioned to think that this is a sin; in another society it might easily be a virtue.' They do not easily distinguish between guilt feelings and sins, and are unfamiliar with the idea of the education of conscience.

Another example of an emotional attitude being expressed in the guise of an intellectual statement is the not infrequent willingness to adopt fundamentalisms of one sort or another. Biblical fundamentalism is frequently accompanied by minor symptoms of anxiety or fear. As Michael Hare Duke points out it is extremely difficult for the young to resign themselves to doubt or confusion. Certainty gives security; it seems intolerable to be left in darkness, and, since God is kind, He would not allow us to get lost in a fog of conditional clauses. It is perplexing for their teachers when young men, who can get a First Class Honours in Physics or Mathematics, can preserve this rigidly closed attitude in some watertight compartment of their minds.

Equally trying is the fundamentalism of the young positivist or empiricist; the closed circle of his tidy logic is usually impregnable but is, as often as not, a defence against the potent but intangible world of feeling. There is obviously a considerable emotional need to assert the total sufficiency of empirical explanations, which leads to assertions like, ' The experience of beauty is just biochemistry '. The prevalence of the scientific myth makes this a much more plausible attitude for the young scientist. The power of technology to get things done is immensely impressive to the young; their trust in it is often an almost religious belief that the troubles of mankind can be healed by scientific enlightenment of which religion has always been the enemy. They can hardly be blamed for this when many eminent adults share and propagate the same illusion.

When we have made allowance for the variety of emotional pressures which may lie behind apparently innocuously intellectual statements we must also recognize that there are genuinely intellectual and ethical problems which trouble the intelligent agnostic boy or girl. Most urgent of these is the problem of suffering, and most perplexing the absence of any rational proofs for the existence of God. There is a group of particular problems around the person of Jesus Christ and the Jewish setting of His ministry, another group around the Christian Church, its worship, morals, and activities, and particularly its exclusive claims. All these problems have a genuinely intellectual content, however loaded they may be in particular cases with emotional undertones, but except in the classroom setting it is difficult to persuade the young to apply themselves to the systematic analysis of each issue rather than indulge in the endless ' discussions ' which usually consist of an extended *argumentum ad hominem* which is seldom profitable. It is a salutary experience for a young man whether believing or agnostic to find his mind and abilities really stretched by a subject which he assumes can have no intellectual content, but it is difficult to do this outside the context of an accepted academic discipline.

Whether in the classroom or outside it we have to face the fact that apologists for the Christian faith are at a disadvantage in winning the confidence of the young in two important respects. In the first place most of them are ministers of religion or obviously establishment laymen. To the young it appears that they have a position to defend at all costs. How often does a clergyman admit the force of an agnostic's case, or even confess that he does not know the answer ? The image that the young have is of a Church which has been on the defensive for four hundred years and is master of infinitely resourceful methods of delay against the forces of light and reason. It seems to me that

religious teaching and discussion at Sixth Form
level must be a *genuinely* open inquiry, in which
the young do not feel that the conclusions are
inevitably prejudged by the commitment of their
teacher. Too often the opposing sides in a discussion are clearly defined before the book has even
been opened, and the teacher feels that he has failed
if he does not have the last word.

The second difficulty facing the Sixth Form
teacher is the effects of the now widely admitted
shortcomings of religious education in the earlier
years at school. The researches of Harold Loukes [1]
and others have underlined the real failure of our
schools to present the young with an account of the
Christian religion which they can recognize as
being in any way related to their own experience
and needs. The rejection of the Christian faith
by many adolescents dates from their experience
of R.I. in the Primary and early Secondary years
of their education. This is no doubt largely due to
the inadequacies of most Agreed Syllabuses, but
may also be due to the fact that in some schools the
subject is taught by non-specialists or even by
teachers who themselves have no sympathy for the
subject at all. By the time most adolescents reach
the Sixth Form they are convinced—often mis-
takenly—that they know what the Christian
religion is, and also that from what they have seen
of it they do not wish to subscribe to it themselves.

How can those who have the job of talking with
young agnostics best approach this far from simple
situation ? Much depends on whether one is
dealing with a group or an individual, and much
on the context of the encounter. I am personally
convinced that the most important single factor is
the emotional attitude of the counsellor to the
group. If he is resentful of their opposition or
nervous of his own failure to alter their attitudes
discussion will seldom be profitable. Similarly he
must be prepared to listen with respect to what
they have to say. The arguments of the young
agnostic are often jejune and uninformed. Nevertheless it is very important that we take them

[1] *New Ground in Christian Education*, S.C.M. Press.

seriously—they may not objectively be of much weight, but they must be of weight to us because they are of importance to the boy or girl who uses them. Of course, we may be absolutely rigorous over matters of undoubted fact, and demand a meticulous approach to evidence. We should not allow a young man to get away with a statement that Jesus Christ never existed. Robert Graves seems currently fashionable as a source of anti-Christian ammunition ; we must insist on a closer attention to the dating of the material he uses than he has allowed himself. When it comes to interpretation and assumption we must try to be much more open in allowing that alternatives do exist. One of the best ways of showing that we do take the sceptical opinions of the young seriously is to make them the substance of our analysis, not with the idea of shredding them to pieces, but rather to try and elucidate alongside them the premisses which often lie unexposed behind their own opinions. It is possible to make a group do this itself to the opinions of its members quite effectively.

In the case of individual counselling it is even harder not to try and force the pace, but there is no doubt in my mind that far more is achieved if the dialogue is conducted on the basis that the counsellor never does more than one third of the talking. With the individual of course the latent emotional pressures are much more easily discerned, and it frequently happens that what began as an intellectual inquiry deepens into a discussion of personal problems, the sensitive handling of which is far more likely to soften a rigid hostility to belief than any amount of argument.

As a broad generalization it may be said that most young people are drawn to the figure of Jesus by an instinctive recognition of His basic goodness. They find the Church incomprehensible or positively distasteful. They are acutely sensitive to personal moral issues but deeply suspicious of anything which seems like dogmatism. They are surprised and intrigued when they find that Christians are in the vanguard of some new and

27

important work like housing in Notting Hill or industrial sociology in Coventry. They have a strong if unrealistic sympathy for the under-privileged. These are the topics around which the Christian apologist is likely to catch and keep their interest and from which it may with patience be possible to lead them to a closer examination of their own attitudes and the claims of faith. A great deal has been achieved if the young leave school with the whole subject still an open issue.

III. The Delinquent in Trouble with the Law—and his Worried Parents

By William L. Carrington, M.D.,
Melbourne, Australia

In the almost unlimited range of requests for
personal help which may come to the Minister
there will certainly be many which relate to some
kind of delinquency. Some of these will involve
delinquents in trouble with the law, and in most,
but not all of them, worried parents will be seeking
help. Not all, because there are adult delinquents,
who are not under parental care and responsibility.
The counselling which may be required in any of
these cases will be considered under four broad
headings: the personal attitudes of the counsellor,
counselling with the parents, counselling with the
delinquent, and counselling with any representative
of the law.

1. *The Personal Attitudes of the Counsellor.* In
dealing with any of the persons involved in the
case of a delinquent in trouble with the law the
Christian Minister may sometimes find himself in
bewildering inner conflict regarding his own attitudes. On the one hand he sees himself as standing
openly in the community for decency and respect
for the law. He is, and is expected to be, a guardian
of private and public morals. On the other hand
he stands for Christian Charity, for good will
without strings, to saint and sinner alike. Until he
can reconcile these two apparently conflicting
rôles he may well find himself confused and inept
in what will always be a most delicate and far
reaching relationship.

Fortunately he has a clear and inescapable
precedent offered to him in the attitude of Jesus
to ' delinquents ' of His time and place, the
publicans and sinners and others like them. It
seems quite clear that He, the champion of righteousness and of public and private morality, deliberately set out to relate closely and lovingly—

and therefore therapeutically—to sinners. Luke 15, surely one of the most beautiful chapters in the Bible, opens with the startled comment of the Pharisees and Scribes, ' This man receiveth sinners and eateth with them '. To eat with anyone was then, and still is in the East, an unmistakable symbol of friendship. It was apparently this expression of amazement by the Pharisees and Scribes, which brought forth from Jesus the three great parables, about the lost sheep, the lost coin, and the lost son—or sons, because the elder brother was also ' lost ' but in a different way.

Jesus showed this good will, this acceptance without strings, to everyone with whom He came into contact, to Zacchaeus, to the mentally ill man named Legion, to the Samaritan woman at the well, to Mary Magdalene, and even to Peter who was to deny Him and to Judas who was to betray Him. He practised fully what He preached about the loving of enemies and doing good to those that hate us.

How can this deeply significant attitude be offered most effectively to the delinquent and where necessary to his troubled parents ? As emphasized in other discussions in this series the first essential in any therapeutic counselling is the kind of listening and commenting which shows acceptance. Acceptance of what ? Obviously not of the destructive behaviour which has brought the delinquent into conflict with the law. The essential foundation for all kinds of therapeutic counselling is the communication of genuine interest in and acceptance of each person and his feelings, even though the counsellor may be unable to understand why the person should feel as he does, even though the counsellor cannot accept his behaviour.

Important as this has been proved to be in individual personal counselling, it is even more important in dealing with the kind of situation implicit in the present subject. Behind the presenting conflict between the delinquent and the Law there will be all kinds of deep, intense, and infinitely complex conflicts, the probability of which needs to be kept constantly in mind by the counsellor. The more obvious of these will of course be between the delinquent and his distressed, perplexed, angry, and possibly remorseful parents. But there may well be deep conflicts between the two parents as well, which may have been influential in the development of the delinquent attitude and behaviour of their son. Beyond these again there will be deep conflicts within each of the people involved, which need to be expressed and worked through in the counselling if the situation is to be used for the most constructive and permanent benefit.

To become involved, often without warning, in such an acute and profound situation, is enough to tax the personal resources of even the most experienced counsellor. How much more difficulty will it present to the less experienced counsellor, whose help is sought urgently and often desperately by people so overcome by feelings of distress that they cannot think clearly. How can he handle the situation without undue risk of harm, and yet without leaving the distressed people disappointed and disillusioned ?

An important requirement is that he should be clear in his own mind about his own function in the situation, and his immediate and ultimate goals. Only then will he be able to preserve a natural calmness and poise without appearing to be callous or lacking in interest or acceptance. Underlying all he may contribute in counselling skill to the situation, his own calmness will have an infectious quality, which will do much to promote and encourage the necessary deliberation when the pent-up feelings have been unburdened. If the counsellor can offer an appropriate combination of compassion and dispassion to each person involved, and at the same time offer them every opportunity and encouragement to ventilate their deeper feelings and conflicts, he will be making a very valuable contribution to the difficult task of bringing the most constructive solution to the complex and distressing problem.

This will often involve a concentrated effort on

the part of the counsellor to resist the temptation to talk, to rush in too soon with possible solutions without giving the deeper and often most vital elements in the problem a chance to come to light. He can take it for granted that each of the people involved will have some resistances against the expression of many of their deeper feelings. Unless the counsellor gives them good opportunities and even in some cases some real encouragement to bring up any deeper elements they may well avoid doing so, and then feel disillusioned because the more superficial approach to the problems has failed to provide the relief and the positive help they hoped for.

The counsellor needs to keep in mind that he is offering first aid counselling, to give the immediate support that is needed, to help clarify the problem, and to make way for any further help needed. These are his goals. How does he set about the actual counselling ?

The experienced counsellor may decide in his wisdom to conduct some of the interviews with the delinquent and his parents together, but the less experienced counsellor may find such group counselling too difficult and even dangerous. He may all the more easily be drawn out of his depth into the turbulent emotional torrents, and thus fail to provide the stabilizing and reconciling influence that is so urgently needed. The people involved may then be left in a state of frustration and despair which may grievously hinder any subsequent counselling by someone with more experience.

In general it may be suggested that when parents are involved they should be interviewed separately from (but not necessarily before) the delinquent. It is generally much easier, particularly for the ' first aid counsellor ', to win the confidence of all parties in this way, and to enable them to unburden their feelings most freely and least harmfully. The counsellor's communications, which will necessarily be different for the parents and the delinquent, may well be more effectively received also in this way. At some point in the whole affair the counsellor may also need to interview a representative of the law.

2. *Interviewing the Worried Parents.* When the parents make the first approach, as often happens, they will naturally be interviewed first. There will usually be no difficulty in getting them to talk about the problem and to give vent to their immediate feelings. The first contribution of the counsellor is a listening ear, sensitive to their intense and often conflicting feelings, and to many deeper undertones of feeling not always expressed directly or even verbally. They may well express anger, frustration, anxiety and apprehensiveness, bewilderment and despair. Whether or not they express directly any sense of guilt or failure it may generally be assumed that they are feeling it. It may be hidden behind a mask of self-righteousness, or the blaming of a scapegoat, or a complaint, 'Why did he do this to us ? ' With all of these feelings there will generally be a strong desire to be helped to get out of the trouble with a minimum of cost or publicity, and perhaps to pull enough strings to save their public and private image from defilement, and their child from the necessary consequences of his actions.

In some cases one or both parents may show bitter hostility directed to the child, and condemn him as ungrateful, incorrigible, and a disgrace to the family. Or they may put a large part of the blame on some external ' scapegoat ', such as a grandparent, a school, or unsuitable companions. The counsellor's function at this point is to encourage the free expression of these feelings, and to draw out from the parents any reasons they may have for feeling as they do. He might do this by some such comment as, ' You feel it was all because he was let down by the school, is that it ? I wonder if you could tell me a little more about that.' It is generally futile at this early stage to try to question the rightness of those views, or to try to argue them out of them, even if they appear illogical and unwarranted. With progressive unburdening of such pent up feelings, however distorted, in an ' accepting ', but not necessarily an ' agreeing ' atmosphere, people often come to see their quite natural evasions and *alibis* more clearly and to face them openly. Too early questioning of such evasions may well put people on the defensive to a still greater extent, and thus push them still further into their defensive blindness.

At a later stage, if the better insights do not seem to be coming, it may be appropriate for the counsellor to help matters on to some extent by some such remark as, ' You have been expressing your concern and distress about your boy and his doings, and I think I can see something of what this has meant to you. I wonder now if you could tell me a little more about yourselves, and perhaps about some of the feelings you may have found it difficult to talk about.' If they respond by saying that they can't see that they could have had any part in the trouble, the counsellor might ask quietly, ' Do you feel happy then about your relationships with the boy over the last few years ? ' If they still attempt to evade the question the counsellor may pursue the matter a little further by such a comment as, ' We have to think about the future as well as the past, and this will depend a lot on your relationship with your son, and possibly on how much you as well as he can profit by this very painful experience. Can you see it in that way ? ' If they are still resistant the counsellor might ask in a quiet kindly way, 'If that is so, how do you feel that I could help you ?' Usually, however, in the setting of better mutual confidence and with sensitive timing, the parents may come to admit that there may have been some inadequate handling of the family relationships on their part, and thus open the way for more fruitful exploration. If they remain unwilling to face up to any possible failure the counsellor might well re-examine his own handling of the situation and ask himself whether he might have failed to offer adequate acceptance or to win their confidence.

As he listens to the parents the counsellor needs to keep alert to any indications of conflict between them in relation to the problem or to the counselling. If, as often happens, there has been any such conflict, it may point to the possibility that it may have had a lot to do with the development of the delinquency. The counsellor may gain a strong hint of such conflict from the way they look at each other, the general attitudes, tone of voice, and points of emphasis as well as from what may be said by either parent. It is generally important for him to pick up and respond to any such indications of conflict, and this portion of the interview may possibly proceed in some such manner as this.

Mother (looking at Father) : ' *I've* seen this coming for a long time. I've warned you repeatedly about John's waywardness, but it was waste of breath ; you never took any notice.'

Counsellor : ' You feel your husband has failed you here ? '

Mother : ' Yes, I do. He has never paid any attention to what I say. And now the thing I've been terrified of has happened ! '

Father : ' I don't think you're quite fair about that, my dear. I haven't always seen eye to eye with you, and I've sometimes thought you were an alarmist. But I have tried to take a responsible interest in John and his doings. Perhaps I've had less ability to see what was coming than you, but it's easy to be wise after the event.'

Mother : ' I still feel that you brushed off my concern about John, and that you were too easygoing with him.'

Counsellor (possibly after allowing some further interaction between them) : ' It seems there have been some differences between you about your attitudes to John, which up till now you've been unable to resolve. Have you been much in conflict about this ? '

Father : ' Yes, I'm afraid we have, and I wish now we had made a better effort to come to some agreement about it. I think perhaps we both need some help here, because I can see that we have to make a better job of it in the future, whatever John has to face just now.'

35

Counsellor (to Mother) : ' How do you feel about that ? '

Mother : ' Yes, I think we both have to learn by our mistakes, and I'll be glad of any further help. I'm a little worried about how we can cope with the responsibility ahead.'

This of course is a very condensed, and rather ' too simple ', version of what might go on in such an interview, but it may serve to illustrate the manner in which the counsellor keeps each parent involved in the discussion and encourages them to come to their own insights.

A further conflict to be alert for is that *within each person*, between love and hate, desire for help and diffidence about seeking it, or between other ' opposite ' feelings. These kinds of ' ambivalence ' are present in everyone, and their recognition and acceptance in counselling is generally of great help in working through the complexities of any problem. It is often a great relief to people to realize that such ambivalences are normal and universal, that any healthy human love will inevitably be accompanied by some real hostility. The counsellor's contribution here is in showing simple acceptance of the ambivalence rather than in any actual assurance that it is normal. For example, when one parent expresses such mixed feelings of love and hate the counsellor might make this kind of comment, ' You love him deeply, but there are times when you feel you could screw his wretched neck ? ' The parent, with some relief, might say, ' Yes, that's right '. If then the normality of such contrary feelings is questioned the counsellor might then assure them of the universal nature of ambivalence in all relationships, from the days of infancy onwards, and the need for acceptance of it.

It may well be that the parents will desire a further interview with the counsellor after he has interviewed the boy, and possibly the representative of the Law. If the counsellor has won their confidence in the first interview any subsequent ones may be relatively easy, and mainly directed to future plans and attitudes, or to referral for any specialized help that may be required.

3. *Interviewing the Delinquent himself.* The same principles will obviously apply here as with all therapeutic interviewing, but it is necessary for the counsellor to be prepared for many different kinds of attitude on the part of the young person. He may present a sullen silence and an unwillingness to co-operate, a vigorous hostile defiance, or, at the other extreme, a shamefaced anxiety. He will probably be ' on guard ' at the beginning, expecting to be condemned in some way. The counsellor's first task is to convey to him that he is genuinely accepted, no matter what he has done, and that the counsellor is interested in him and his feelings. The ' opening gambit ' is of great importance here, as in all counselling, but especially with a person in conflict with constituted authority.

The counsellor's greeting needs to be simple, sincere, and warm, accompanied by a natural handshake, the counsellor looking at him naturally and with a pleasant open expression, and asking him to make himself comfortable. He may offer an opening observation, such as, ' Well, it seems you're in a tough spot for the moment ; would you like to tell me something of how you feel about it all, and perhaps then we can put our heads together and see what might be done about it '. If the boy says nothing, this can be shown to be accepted by such a remark as ' You find it hard to talk about ? ' or, if the boy appears to be sullen and hostile, ' You find it hard to trust anyone after what has happened ? '

The boy should be encouraged to unburden all his feelings, however hostile, and the counsellor's response should be a simple ' reflecting ' one, such as ' You feel pretty sore about the way you've been treated ? ' or ' It's hard to understand why so and so took that attitude ? ' This shows acceptance but not agreement or condoning.

As the feelings are unburdened the counsellor can turn the discussion towards the underlying factors, and ask, ' How did you get involved in this ? What did it do for you ? ' Most behaviour problems can be understood as a rather crude and often impulsive effort of a person to solve some problem that is real to him, even though it may not be realized as such by others. The counsellor hopes to be able to look with him at the problem, and possibly later to try to help him find more socially acceptable ways of dealing with it. The problems will probably be mainly concerned with relationships and ambivalences. They may involve parents, schoolmasters, other authority figures, such as foremen at work, gang leaders, siblings, companions, or girl friends. Sometimes ministers come into the picture. The counsellor should attempt quietly and patiently to draw out the boy's feelings and attitudes to himself and to all the significant people to whom he relates, and to look for and work through the ambivalences. He will also need to look with the boy at the boy's feelings about what penalty might be imposed on him, the spirit in which he might be willing to ' take his medicine ' and the extent to which he might be helped to profit by the experience.

An important part of the discussion will be that which is directed to his future attitudes to his parents, and his ideas about their future attitudes to him. It may be necessary to remind him at some point that until he is twenty-one they are legally responsible for him, and that if he is unable for a time to earn his living, he may be financially dependent on them. If he feels they are over-possessive, rejecting, indifferent, or in gross conflict between themselves, the need for further help towards better mutual understanding and reconciliation may be explored and its value emphasized.

The interview should end if possible on a reasonably positive note, and the continuing interest of the counsellor and an invitation for any further interviews expressed. In many cases the delinquent will be released on a bond, and the possible implications of this should be discussed.

4. *Interviewing the Representative of the Law.* If this happens, it may involve a policeman, a lawyer, a probation officer, or in some cases possibly a

magistrate. The counsellor will be anxious to know the attitude of such people to the offence and the possible penalty, and his opinions may be sought on the possibilities of reformation and the most helpful way of promoting the future ' law abiding ' behaviour of the boy. The counsellor needs to be cautious in any ' prophetic ' statement, but he may well suggest what in his opinion would best encourage the reformation, whether it can be expected with the boy left under his parents' care, with or without the assistance of a probation officer, or whether some kind of institutional care may be necessary. The decision about these matters will be the responsibility of the courts, but the opinions of the counsellor, and any specialist who may be brought in, will often be welcomed by the court.

In a situation such as this the usual practice of confidentiality may have to be modified to some extent, but it is helpful if the counsellor can be open with each person about the extent of possible disclosures, and can allow the person involved to choose whether he will communicate anything he may not wish disclosed. The implications of any non-communication will need to be discussed in such cases, but the counsellor is ' playing fair ' with all parties in this way.

Even with ' first aid ' counselling there may be continuing interviews with one or more people at a time, and many more things will come up for discussion, particularly the important practical matters of reconciling broken relationships, the meaning of forgiveness, and the recognition that the honest acceptance of failure can open the way to new and more promising beginnings. It is impossible to set limits to ' first aid ' counselling, or indeed to any counselling project, but an attempt has been made to offer some guiding principles and methods in this delicate and difficult, but very important, counselling service.

IV. The Pregnant Single Girl and Her Parents

By the Reverend Kenneth G. Greet,
Secretary of The Department of Christian
Citizenship of the Methodist Church,
Westminster

Monica Furlong in her book *With Love to the Church* says ' one of the oddest, most unattractive aspects of organized Christianity is its arrogance, its blind certainty that what it says and does is right and brooks no alternative point of view '.[1] However much the Church may have deserved this stricture in the past, and it would not be difficult to think of examples of unseemly arrogance, the present indications are that the Church is less concerned to stand over against the world in judgment, and more anxious to understand its problems so that solutions may be found.

This change in attitude is nowhere more evident than in our dealings with the unmarried mother. In fairness it should be said that the change is even more noticeable in society generally than in the Church itself for there have always been Christians with a deep and practical compassion for the single pregnant girl.

The simple statement that there is now a more kindly and helpful attitude in society towards the unmarried mother must, however, be qualified. Her situation, always a difficult one, is still in many instances made more agonizing than it need be. Thomas Coram's Foundling Hospital, opened in 1741, was delayed for twenty years by the argument that the giving of help to unmarried mothers encourages vice. This is an argument that is still to be heard to-day, unsupported, it need hardly be said, by any sort of evidence.

The reservations which some people have about treating the pregnant single girl kindly are often

[1] *With Love to the Church*, Monica Furlong (Hodder), 23.

linked, superficially at any rate, with a concern about the alleged deterioration of morals in this century. In fact, harsh judgments are often the result of a misreading of what is actually happening to our society ; and they may also be related to guilt complexes and inhibitions in the personality of those who judge. It is very important that Christians, especially those who undertake pastoral counselling, should not swallow uncritically the popular view that morals, particularly within the sexual sphere, are going to the dogs. The Schofield Report [1] is the most thorough investigation of the sexual behaviour of young people yet undertaken in Great Britain. It says : ' It is impossible to say how the behaviour of to-day's generation compares with that of the past ', but goes on to express the judgment that ' a survey undertaken in the twenties might not have reached results widely different from those of today '.

This is surely a wise conclusion. The illegitimacy rate in this country has fluctuated, but if a long enough period is reviewed, has remained surprisingly constant. At the present time about one baby in seven is conceived out of wedlock and one in fourteen is illegitimate. The number of illegitimate children born annually in England and Wales is about 50,000. Recent years have seen an increase in the number of illegitimate births, particularly to younger girls. In England and Wales the number of illegitimate live births to girls of fifteen and under was 297 in 1957 and 1,111 in 1962. The corresponding figures for girls of sixteen and under were 924 in 1957 and 2,870 in 1962. These numbers may well have been affected by several factors which have little directly to do with morals. One is the increase in the number of young people in this age group as a result of the post-war bulge in the birth-rate ; another is the fact of earlier physical maturity ; and yet another is the arrival in this country of large numbers of Commonwealth immigrants whose pattern of family life differs from our own.

[1] *The Sexual Behaviour of Young People*, Michael Schofield (Longmans).

The really significant statistics, however, are those which deal with the infantile mortality rates. In 1913 over 200 illegitimate babies in every 1,000 died during the first year of life. This was double the number of casualties among legitimate babies. At the present time the mortality rate among illegitimate babies is 25 in every 1,000—only slightly higher than the figure of 21 in every 1,000 for legitimate babies. No other single fact speaks more eloquently of the change in social attitudes and public caring.

The concern of society for the illegitimate child has been shown in a number of enlightened legislative enactments. The Legitimacy Acts of 1926 and 1959 enable the child to be legitimized by the subsequent marriage of his parents. A shortened form of birth certificate is available which does not refer to the fact of illegitimacy. The 1959 Act gives the father rights of custody and access in appropriate cases. There are still, however, residual legal disabilities in respect of the illegitimate child which need to be removed. About one-third of the illegitimate children are born to co-habiting parents. Changes in the divorce law at present under discussion would allow many of these couples to marry and so legitimize their children. Only in about ten per cent. of illegitimacy cases is an affiliation order made (the maximum award which can be made under such an order is fifty shillings). The procedure whereby the mother has to go to court to apply for the order to be made is inappropriate. There is a need for family courts in which matters could be settled between the parties on an informal basis. In Denmark the State makes an allowance and recovers it from the father.

It is now being recognized that the unmarried mother must be seen as part of a more general problem—that of the unsupported mother. There are more than half a million unsupported mothers in Britain : some unmarried, some widowed, some divorced, and some deserted by their husbands. The very real needs of this considerable group of persons have not been sufficiently considered.

One of the most pressing needs of all, to which it is hoped Housing Associations will increasingly turn their attention, is for special housing accommodation.

This article is mainly concerned with the pastoral approach to the single pregnant girl and her parents. It seemed necessary, however, first of all to look briefly at the social problem which illegitimacy presents, and the general trends in public approach and attitude towards it at the present time. If compassion is one indispensable quality in the counsellor, knowledge is also extremely valuable.

Those who study social statistics need constantly to be reminded that behind the paper figures stand human figures. This becomes painfully clear when one of them materializes at our front door, in the shape of a pregnant unmarried girl, or more often, perhaps, her mother.

The first thing to remember is that no two cases are precisely the same. Very frequently the girl comes from a deprived background ; she has been starved of affection and lacks a sense of security. Often, with almost uncanny precision, she seems to have been re-enacting the circumstances of her own birth. But this does not apply in every case. The kind of advice the counsellor gives will depend very much on his assessment of the total situation. His initial advice will usually be that no decisions should be hurriedly taken. He himself will need time to acquaint himself with the details. He must talk with the girl, but at first only enough to encourage her to talk to him. He wants to establish a relationship of confidence and he wants to understand her feelings. In most cases those feelings will fluctuate a great deal, especially when the question of the baby's future is discussed.

The relationship between the girl and the father of her child is obviously of great importance. It may be one of indifference or even hostility. She may not be sure who the father is, or there may be a real love between the couple, even an intention to marry. If the couple love one another but the

43

fellow is too young to be able to support the girl, it may be possible, rather than resorting to the court, for a satisfactory private agreement to be made between the two of them. The saddest circumstance is often where the girl loves the fellow but her love is not returned.

The unmarried father or father-to-be often has great needs. Wherever possible he needs to be brought into the picture. The Christian counsellor has a responsibility for him, though this is often difficult to discharge because the putative father may be elusive or unwilling to accept his share of the burden. If marriage is not contemplated, the acceptance by the father of the child of proper financial responsibility is important for the girl, but may also be important for the fellow.

The relationship between the girl and her parents is also of fundamental importance. Some parents rise magnificently to the heavy responsibilities thrust upon them by their daughter's pregnancy ; the response of others is less helpful. The counsellor may need to exercise great tact and wisdom in helping parents and daughter to a deeper level of mutual understanding. The initial news of the pregnancy will often have come as a tremendous shock to all involved. The fact that the Christian pastor can look non-judgmentally at the situation may help to alleviate the sense of isolation which many families feel, and also to mitigate the spirit of condemnation which righteous people often feel when confronted with sexual misconduct. Sometimes social workers do not give the grandparents time to adjust to the fact that they have an out-of-wedlock grandchild. Very often, after a time, grandparents who were inclined to be hostile will come to accept the situation and the child.

The very fact that the pastor is there, prepared to listen and understand, will, in itself, be a great help. But the more effective he proves as a friend, the more he will be looked to for practical advice. He will almost certainly want to put the girl in touch with the appropriate social worker. The earlier this is done the better. Also the girl should be referred to a doctor or an ante-natal clinic as early as possible in her pregnancy so that her health and that of the coming child may be safeguarded. The pastor should acquaint himself with the range of social services for the unmarried mother available in his area.

What are the options, to be considered in the light of the circumstances pertaining to the individual case ? The first, and in many cases, most satisfactory solution, is that the girl should marry the man. In 1960, 104,253 children were conceived out of wedlock and 60,972 of these had parents who married before the birth. No doubt many of these marriages took place in registry offices. Some couples who may have intended to marry in Church may have decided to go to the registry office instead. Others may have married in Church without telling the parson. But if the parson is aware of the situation, and if he is asked to marry the couple, what should be his response ? Everything depends on the attitude of the couple. A ' shot-gun ' marriage can never be Christian (this term is used to describe a union entered into reluctantly, under pressure, for the sake of respectability). It is much better that the couple should remain unmarried than that they enter into a marriage which may well end presently in divorce. (Incidentally, the commendable modern reluctance to force young people to marry necessarily increases the illegitimacy returns.) If there is real love between the girl and the man, by all means let them be married in Church. Like all other men and women who stand before the altar, they are sinners. Their behaviour has been irresponsible : they now have the chance to atone by accepting the larger responsibilities that come with permanent union and parenthood.

Where an unmarried couple expecting a child are in love and desire to marry the situation is often complicated by their youthfulness and lack of adequate means. One or both of them may still be in training for the work they intend to do. It is impossible to lay down any standard solutions to their perplexities. Marriages contracted at a very early age before the parties have reached

45

some degree of maturity are obviously at risk. In cases where parents are co-operative, it may be wise to wait until the young man is earning enough to offer his wife and child some measure of security. If there is a real relationship between the couple, it is wrong to forbid them to see each other. They will need each other, especially during the period of pregnancy. The man will often have his own anxieties and fears. Though it is often assumed that the man is always to blame, if we are talking in terms of blame, it should be recognized that sometimes it is the girl who has made the running.

We must next consider the case of the girl who will not, for one reason or another, marry the father of her child. Assuming that the baby is born alive and well, the immediate question is whether the mother shall keep her child or not. It is more and more accepted that everything possible should be done to enable the mother to keep her child, though not every one takes this view. Often, of course, it is the mothers who are least able to cope who most passionately desire to keep their children. If the mother comes from a poor background and if she has known little of love in her life, the baby may be all she has to love. Such mothers, however, often need a tremendous amount of help. Far too often that help is not forthcoming with the result that they struggle on for a time but are beaten in the end and their child has to be taken into care. In Denmark, where the problem is treated very seriously, over ninety per cent. of unmarried mothers keep their children. Some, however, criticize the Danish system as being too impersonal.

Whether the mother is likely to keep her baby or not, it may be best for her to go away from home for the confinement. This can only be decided in the light of the home situation. There are about one hundred and seventy-four mother and baby homes in England and Wales. A girl may be required to stay for a minimum period of six weeks before the birth of her baby, and for a similar period after—a rule which sometimes seems to be applied rather too rigidly. An alternative to going to a home is a sympathetic relative who will undertake to care for the girl until her child is born.

Some girls make up their minds about the main issue of keeping or parting with the child before the baby is born. For others there is an agony of uncertainty and indecision, and this may be increased when the baby has actually arrived.

Two comments at this point are of great importance. The first is that the child must never be made part of a plan for somebody else : the interests of the child must be paramount. The second comment is that the strain on the mother of parting with her baby must never be underestimated. There is often a well-intentioned effort on the part of family and friends to leave the incident behind as quickly as possible and encourage the girl to forget all about it. But her sorrow and emptiness may be even more poignant than that of someone mourning a death. She must be allowed to acknowledge and express her grief.

If the unmarried mother decides to keep her child, and if she is not able to live with her parents, the big problem, as already mentioned, will often be that of suitable accommodation. Some local authorities are willing to place unmarried mothers on their housing lists, and a few have made special housing arrangements. Most of the initiative in providing flatlets or bed-sitting-rooms, however, has come from voluntary organizations, and there is need for much more to be done. Christians should be encouraged to let rooms or flats to unmarried women and their children on the same basis as they would normally let them to any one else. The unmarried mother is entitled to the same maternity benefits as the married woman and should be able to afford a reasonable rent. Some girls accept posts in residential jobs where they can take their baby. This can be more demanding than they often realize, and for the intelligent girl, mentally restrictive after a time.

If a decision is made to have the baby adopted,

47

it is very important that the arrangements should be made either by one of the registered Adoption Societies or through the Children's Department of the Local Authority. Attempts to arrange matters by well-intentioned amateurs can prove disastrous. Although it is sometimes assumed that the mother who intends to have her baby adopted should be spared the torment of seeing her child, there is need for flexibility in this regard. The young mother needs the understanding and advice of some one who is aware of the uncertainties which fill her mind. The essential thing is that she should be led to decisions which she feels in her own heart she can honour. Some mothers who have decided during pregnancy to have the baby adopted, alter their minds when the baby has arrived.

The demand for long-term fostering far exceeds the supply and Local Authorities and other organizations continually appeal for people who are willing to open their home to a little child. This fact constitutes a challenge to Christians. Many foster mothers find it more acceptable to take 'short-term' babies (those mainly who are later to be adopted) as they are afraid of becoming too fond of the child. The Thomas Coram Home tries to help the uncertain or struggling girl until she reaches the point of decision or the way opens for her to take full control of her little one.

If there is reason to hope that the mother will be able, after a period, to assume full responsibility for her child though unable to do so immediately, the possibility of finding suitable foster parents should be considered rather than that of having the child adopted.

There is one other option which may come within the sphere of practical possibility if certain proposals relating to the law on abortion are enacted by Parliament. A limited number of legal abortions are performed every year under the case law which provides that no offence has been committed if the doctor acted in good faith with the sole intention of preserving the life of the mother. For some time it has been widely felt that this case law should become statute law. But it has been further argued that the grounds of legal abortion should be extended to include cases where there is a grave risk that the child will be severely abnormal ; cases where a sexual offence, such as rape, has been committed ; and cases where the mother is, or believes herself to be, incapable of bearing a child, or another child, as the case may be.

If the law is amended along the lines proposed in the measure currently before Parliament (Mr. David Steel's ' Medical Termination of Pregnancy Bill '), quite obviously the new provisions would cover many of the cases of unmarried mothers about whom we have been thinking. Some of the most difficult cases are those of young girls who are pregnant under the age of sixteen. They would presumably be covered by a clause which allows abortion if a sexual offence has been committed. If the so-called ' social clause ' should pass into law, this would cover the cases of mothers who are often desperately convinced that they cannot continue with the pregnancy. (Many of these at the moment take the law into their own hands and resort to the unskilled illegal operator.)

This is not the place to enter into the complexities of the debate on abortion. Every man must follow the dictates of his conscience (and this applies particularly in this case to the doctors). It should be said, however, that those who have sponsored this particular amendment of the law have argued that it would encourage women contemplating abortion to take their problem to a competent adviser, instead of running off to the back-street abortionist. At the moment if the counsellor ever finds himself confronted with the desperate woman who wants to get rid of the foetus, unless there is a clear medical indication to the contrary, he will advise against such action. He may give this advice not only because the law forbids such abortion, but also because his conscience condemns it. If the law should be amended in the way indicated, this is bound to increase the demands made upon the counsellor. He will have the more earnestly to search his own conscience, facing the fact, as he must do, that for the woman before him, the field of choice has been widened.

At the end of this brief survey of a large and complex problem, it may be well to remind ourselves of a fact that applies to all the work we do in an attempt to help people faced with problems. The effectiveness of the counsellor depends to a great extent on his contact with the experts who can provide the knowledge and the service which particular cases may demand. So far as the unmarried mother is concerned, those experts include the child welfare and moral welfare workers, the doctor and the maternity services, and the adoption societies. And no article on this subject would be complete which did not refer to the work of the National Council for the Unmarried Mother and Her Child, 255 Kentish Town Road, London, N.W.5, from whom suggestions for further reading can be obtained.

V. Where a Marriage Breakdown is Threatened

BY WILLIAM L. CARRINGTON, M.D.,
MELBOURNE, AUSTRALIA

THE minister (or layman) may be first acquainted with the threatened breakdown of a marriage indirectly when he is approached by a third person on behalf of, or possibly without the knowledge of, the two partners ; or because of some trouble affecting the children of the marriage. Or he may come into direct contact with it through an approach by one or both partners or by meeting the situation in his visiting or in a social contact. His early strategy will naturally depend on which of these initial approaches are made.

When the initial approach is from a third person the minister will need first to know whether the partners are aware of this action, and if so whether they approve of it. He must decide whether it would be most appropriate for him to call on them or to suggest that they be invited to come to him for counselling. The minister is in a more favoured position to call on people than is any other professional helper, especially if the partners are members of his church or his denomination. If he decides to call on them, his best approach, after the usual greeting, is a simple statement that he has heard that things are not happy between them, and an offer of help which leaves the person or the couple free to decline. If the offer is accepted he might feel it appropriate to conduct the initial interview there and then, but subsequent interviews are generally best conducted in his study or some other place in which his counselling may be carried out. When people come in this way for counselling their actual coming is valuable as a gesture of active participation in the reconciling work.

In some cases it may appear more appropriate for the minister to invite the couple by letter, or to allow the third person to convey the invitation. In such cases the minister may need to satisfy himself that a written invitation would be more acceptable than a personal call, or that the third person would not unwittingly misrepresent the nature and goals of the counselling. For this purpose it may be advisable to have some discussion with him about his concepts of counselling and his relationship with the couple.

If the minister's first contact with the situation is through some trouble affecting the children of the marriage he will inevitably ask to see the parents, who may not fully realize that the children's difficulties are related to any conflict between them, or if they do they may not be anxious to discuss it. In either case the Counsellor will invite them to give an account of the trouble, showing full acceptance of their feelings and encouraging the fullest expression of them. When they have unburdened their feelings about the children's behaviour the Counsellor might ask them (or the one who comes) about their relationships with each other. If there seems to be any question in their minds about the relevance of this to any difficulties with their children it may be appropriate for the Counsellor to say that many such troubles are at least intensified by difficulties and conflicts in and between the parents, and often very closely related to them. He might also say that any attempt to help children in such difficulties is unlikely to succeed unless the home atmosphere can support the Counsellor's efforts. Before any programme of counselling or psychotherapy is offered to a disturbed or ' problem ' child or children it is necessary to make it clear to the parents that they need to be involved to a considerable extent.

By defining the situation in this way at the beginning it may be possible to make close enough contact with the marital conflict, and to strengthen the motivation of the parents to participate in counselling.

If one or both partners in the marital disturbance are brought into contact with the Counsellor either directly or through one of these 'pre-counselling' situations the way is open for the real process of marriage counselling to begin.

It needs to be emphasized at this point that the first impressions the two partners gain of the Counsellor and the counselling process are vitally important, and worthy of the most careful attention.

In particular the Counsellor needs to be interested, and to show interest in the feelings of the person or persons about coming for help and participating in counselling, and also in their feelings about their marriage and their motivation for working at it. Many people in this kind of situation are quite embarrassed about admitting their difficulties and failures, or discussing their intimate affairs with another person, possibly even more so when the person happens to be their minister. Men generally feel this more than women, or at least appear to be less willing to participate unless they have been 'deserted'. If the partners feel that the Counsellor is sensitive to such feelings and accepts them sympathetically and non-judgmentally they are more likely to feel free to co-operate in the counselling.

The general handling of the counselling will differ to some extent according to whether the first direct contact is with one partner or with both together.

If the initial contact is with both it is generally best to begin at least as a joint interview. In some cases it may even be a family interview at the beginning. As the main focus of marriage counselling is on the relationships between the people concerned, it is of some value to see, hear, and feel their interaction as early as possible in the counselling. The Counsellor will have an opportunity to observe the way in which they look at each other and at him, and to gain some idea of the amount of tension between them, which will probably be quite noticeable in this case of a marriage at breaking-point. He will also notice which one seems to be taking most of the initiative and doing most of the talking.

The decision as to whether to allow the joint interview to proceed or whether to offer them separate interviews at this stage will depend on a number of considerations. The inexperienced Counsellor may find it difficult to avoid being drawn into the interaction in such a manner in a joint interview that he cannot avoid taking sides, or he may be unable to tolerate the intense hostility that may be expressed, or uncertain as to how far he can allow one partner to be persecuted. On the other hand, one or both partners may wish to have an opportunity to talk with the Counsellor alone, or may feel more able to express their feelings without the presence of the other partner. This wish may be expressed verbally, but sometimes the partner may feel diffident about this and express it more by the non-verbal gesture of sitting with head bowed and taking no part in the discussion.

In such cases, after about five minutes of the joint interview, during which many of these aspects of the interaction have become evident, the Counsellor might offer such a remark as, ' People often feel better able to discuss these difficulties separately rather than together with a Counsellor at this stage. Would either of you feel easier if we handle it in that way ? '. One partner, often the more retiring one, will often say ' Yes ', or show acceptance of the idea by a nod of the head. In that case the Counsellor might suggest, preferably to the more active or aggressive partner, ' Perhaps you could retire for a little while, and I shall be glad to hear something of your feelings about it then '.

If the two partners appear to prefer to carry on together it is generally best to allow them to do so, even if the level of hostility is high. It may be remembered that they have probably become accustomed to a high level of hostility, and more able to tolerate it than the Counsellor may assume. But whatever they or the Counsellor decide at this interview it is generally desirable to offer each partner a private interview at some time in the course of any continued counselling.

If one partner has retired to another room the Counsellor may need to give some encouragement to the one who has remained. This might be achieved by such a remark as, ' I imagine you have been feeling very troubled about the whole situation '. It may be of help at some early stage to assure the person that everything he says will be held in strictest confidence, even from the other partner. This will often lead to freer discussion, and it is most important that it should be strictly observed by the Counsellor. He may sometimes attempt to interpret some of the needs of one partner to the other, usually in the form of a question, such as ' Do you think she might be needing a little more appreciation at times ? '. But ' tale bearing ' has no place in counselling.

Before leaving these questions of strategy some consideration may be given to another common problem in the Counsellor's handling of the two partners, the way in which the second partner may be invited when only one partner comes for help or can be seen at the beginning. Assuming that the two partners are still living in the same house (the present discussion is about a threatened breakdown) the Counsellor will first need to know from the presenting partner whether or not the other one knows of this approach. If not, the Counsellor might ask how the person feels about telling him. If she (assuming the first contact is with the wife) is in any doubt about this it may be wise to go on counselling with her until she can feel able to tell her husband about coming. In such cases the counselling should not be conducted at her home.

If she has told her husband about coming, or undertakes to do so, the way is then open for him to be invited to come for an interview, or in certain cases to be called on by the minister, as long as the wife's consent for such an invitation has been obtained. It is generally unwise to allow the invitation to be given by the wife. When the partners are in severe conflict it is possible that her husband will reject it on principle. Some men are too proud to play ' second fiddle ' to their wives, even when they are in a distressing situation. In some cases the minister may feel able to call on the husband to offer his help, but it is important then to leave it open for the husband to reject the offer if he chooses to do so. In many cases the most helpful approach to the second partner is by letter, in which the opportunity can be taken to convey to him something of the Counsellor's own attitude and the nature of the counselling. A helpful kind of letter would be :

Dear Mr. ——

As you probably know, your wife has sought help from me in the situation that has arisen in your marriage. I think I might be of more help if I could have an opportunity to hear something of how you feel about it all. If you can manage to come for a discussion I would be happy to see you, and I would be glad if you would make a suitable appointment (or let me know when I could call on you or meet you).

With best wishes, Yours sincerely, ——

If such a husband comes, unless he knows the Counsellor well, he may have many doubts as to how he will be received, in spite of the letter which expresses interest in how he feels about it. He may feel worried about what his wife has said about him, and to some extent ' on guard ' in his first approach to the Counsellor. The ' opening gambit ' in the first interview with him is therefore of the greatest importance. A useful approach by the Counsellor might carry on the attitude expressed in the letter in some such manner as, ' Good afternoon, Mr. ——, I'm glad you were able to come. I guess you've been having a lot of worry about this whole business '. This will easily lead on to the invitation to a full expression of his feelings, and in most cases the Counsellor will feel a progressive relaxing of the husband's tension.

If the letter is ignored, or if the invitation is declined by letter or telephone, it is unwise for the Counsellor to exert any further pressure on him. If he has declined the invitation a further letter may be in order, accepting this with regret and stating that he would be welcome at any time in the future if he should wish to come.

These initial strategies are of great importance whether the minister is merely offering ' first aid counselling ' with the idea of referral to someone else, or is considering a fuller service of more extended counselling. The first impressions gained by the troubled people are quite crucial for the whole counselling process, especially when the two partners have reached the point of despair (or near despair) about the future of their marriage. If through a discouraging initial approach they give up the attempt the damage may well be irreparable. If, on the other hand, they discover that their feelings are accepted with genuine concern it may well be that their flickering hopes will be sustained and reinvigorated, so that whoever carries on with the counselling will have the best chance to assist them to work through to a deep and lasting reconciliation. Even if an inadequate initial approach does not lead them to give up the effort, it may be quite difficult to make up for it in later counselling.

Having considered some of the ways by which this delicate and fragile situation may be handled at the beginning, it is now appropriate to consider the conduct of the initial interview with either husband or wife. It is important in this for the Counsellor to resist any temptation to provide ' solutions ', however strongly and urgently he may be urged by the partners to do so. They will probably have suffered already from plenty of well-meant and apparently ' reasonable ' advice, mostly beyond their ability to act on. There are deep elements in most of these conflicts, of which the partners are largely unaware, and until some of these elements can be given the opportunity to reveal themselves any ' solution ' will be likely to be superficial and temporary, and the relapse in such cases will only add to the deep despair. At some point in the interview it may be necessary to offer some information about what counselling sets out to do : to help each partner to help himself, to come to clearer understanding of what has been happening between them and within each of them, so that they can more adequately deal with their situation and decide for themselves what they can best do about it.

It is clear from this that in any sequence of counselling interviews for marital disorder there are various levels of ' depth ' to which the counselling may go. It is helpful for the Counsellor to recognize these and to have a good idea at any time how deeply the counselling is going. These levels in approximate order of depth may be formulated as follows :

1. Listening, with or without appropriate comments.
2. Clarification of the Interaction as it is at present.
3. Information Giving, for assistance in the clarification.
4. Assistance in Problem Solving in the ' here and now '.
5. Relating present feelings, actions, and interactions to past feelings and experiences in the family of origin or with significant people.

This is generally about as deeply as the Marriage Counsellor as distinct from the psychotherapist will generally allow the counselling to go. The psychotherapist, of course, is likely to venture further into the inner dynamics of the individual person, with the help of free association, discussion of dreams, and the specific therapeutic use of the transference situation. Some of these elements may enter the marriage counselling at times, but they are not deliberately used. It is not the rôle of the Marriage Counsellor as such to ' cure ' a neurotic person.

These five levels of counselling may now be considered briefly in the order given.

1. *Listening*. The first and probably the most important rôle of the Counsellor is to be a good listener, one who can encourage the troubled person or persons to unburden their feelings fully and freely. While people are in the grip of disturbing feelings they cannot ' see ', and even the best advice and reasoning are likely to be futile

and even harmful, increasing the despair. The good listener allows the person to go on talking, and at appropriate times offers a brief comment which conveys interest in and acceptance of the *feelings* being expressed, rather than the facts. For example, when the person has given an account of some cruel behaviour on the part of a marriage partner the Counsellor's comment might be, ' It was very upsetting to you ', rather than ' What happened then ? ' or ' What did you do about it ? '. Even when the person expresses complete despair the Counsellor will help best as a rule by showing acceptance of this by such a comment as, ' You've reached the end of your tether ' or ' You can't see any way out of the situation '. In the face of a demand for advice, such as, ' What can I do ? ', the Counsellor might suggest, ' Perhaps if we could look together at some other aspects of the complex problem we might be able to understand it better and see some light about what may be helpful '.

2. *Clarification.* As the person pours out his feelings and his attitudes to the partner's behaviour the Counsellor will have an opportunity to gain some impressions of underlying elements in the problem. He will perceive some kind of pattern as he becomes aware of what the various experiences mean to the person, some ' uncritical assumptions ', such as ' He ought to behave the way I expect ', some emotional needs which are being unfulfilled, and some rôle perceptions and expectations which may appear unrealistic, or at least at variance with those of the partner. As these and other relevant habitual attitudes are perceived by the Counsellor his best response is generally to offer them to the person in an unthreatening ' questioning comment, ' such as, ' From what you've been saying it sounds as if you've been expecting your husband to fit in with your ideas and he has been expecting you to fit in with his, is that it ? '. If this clarification is accepted the Counsellor's next approach is not the negative one, ' But you can't expect him to do that ', but rather an attempt at further clarification, ' I wonder why you are expecting

that ', or ' Do you think that's worth some further consideration ? '. In such a manner as this the Counsellor attempts to be a kind of ' psychic mirror ' in which the person can gradually achieve a more objective view of himself and of the whole conflict. Another helpful type of question at an appropriate point may be, ' What do you think your partner would be saying about this if he were here ? ', as long as any hostile retort can be accepted, by such comment as ' You wouldn't trust him to face up to it '.

3. *Information Giving.* At many points in the interview there may be a need for specific information to assist in the process of clarification, on such matters as the differences in attitudes of men and women to sex, love, and possibly the handling of children. It is necessary to distinguish between information giving and advice ; and even information can sometimes be given in questioning form, which encourages the person to think and to participate more actively. Such a question as, ' Do you think the conflict here might partly depend on the fact that women tend to think and feel differently about these things ? '.

4. *Assistance in Problem Solving in the ' here and now '.* Toward the end of any interview it is often of great help if the Counsellor can offer the person or persons a brief summary of what has emerged in the interview and invite comments on it. For example, ' From what you've been saying it seems that you've been deeply upset by your husband's attitude, and all your efforts to get him to be different or even to talk things over with you have been futile. But you seem to have come to some realization that he may have been feeling pretty bewildered and anxious too, even if he hasn't let on about it. Is that the way you see it ? ' Such a summary leaves it open for the person to correct any misunderstandings without disturbing the ' rapport ', and also opens the way for some suggestions for further thought and action. The counsellor may go on from here with something constructive, such as, ' It looks as if there's a need for better communication between you, and yet

that's what you've found so difficult. As you see it now, can you see any way of showing your understanding of his feelings ? Or could you encourage him to tell you more about them and show him that you are interested in them and ready to accept them ? ' If there has been a marked difference in rôle perceptions and expectations a suggestion that they might do some work on this may be in order.

5. *Relating present feelings, actions, and inter-actions with past feelings and experiences* would generally take the counselling rather beyond ' first aid ', but it may be valuable even in first-aid counselling at times. It is particularly helpful in counselling when the more superficial approaches fail to relieve the ' stalemate ', when people can't resolve their conflicts or restore communications. It is introduced generally in one of two ways. ' Does this feeling remind you of anything you may have felt with either parent or anyone else as you grew up, a brother or sister, aunt or uncle ? ' or ' Now I've heard about your problem I wonder if you could tell me something about yourself and your earlier life '. Many of the apparently un-warranted or unreasonable attitudes and actions in the intimate relationships of marriage and parenthood can be seen and better understood as ' carry-overs ' from *unresolved* emotional tensions, conflicts, and traumatic experiences in the family of origin or with other significant people. Some of these may be difficult for the person to remember or at least to talk about, and this is where skilled counselling and a good therapeutic relationship are important. Even when they are talked out and related to the present difficulties some patient and persistent ' working through ' may be necessary. But in many cases the conflict will not be resolved until some of these deeper underlying factors can be brought to light and dealt with.

Finally, as the ' first-aid counselling ' ap-proaches its possible conclusion it is necessary for the Counsellor to take some trouble to plan out any future procedure with the person or persons, and to try to preserve and encourage their motivation for going on working at it. If a referral seems desirable it is important to give the people a chance to express their feelings about it and to suggest any alternatives. A referral might be suggested by such a comment as ' I think we might need some special help in this area (for example, a sexual difficulty or conflict), and I think it would be more in the field of work of X than in mine. How would you feel about seeing him if I gave you a letter of referral to him ? '

Referral may be partial, about certain specific aspects of the problem, or total, for the full counselling help, and in either case it needs careful and patient handling. Alternatively, it may be necessary or desirable for the first-aid counsellor to go on with the counselling, particularly if no other help is available or acceptable. In such cases any interviews should be concluded on a positive note as far as possible, with some definite suggestions for further work at some aspect of the problem and a definite invitation for further appointments.

In all cases it is desirable for the Counsellor to write a summary of the main details of the case after each interview, and to keep all such records in a safe place and in strictest confidence.

If the emergency is handled in the manner described, necessarily in all too brief terms, the Counsellor may well have the privilege of seeing some most dramatic reconciliations in what may have appeared almost hopeless marital conflicts. The results of this on the partners and on their children are beyond assessment.

VI. The Mother whose Children are now grown up and no longer need her as once they did

By William L. Carrington, M.D.,
Melbourne, Australia

' Change,' as Matthew Arnold once observed, ' doth unknit the tranquil strength of men.' When it involves the partial or complete loss of something or someone cherished and valued it may well bring a grief reaction comparable to that following bereavement, which will be discussed from the point of view of first aid counselling in a later contribution to this series.

In the particular situation of the mother who has suddenly come to the unwelcome realization that her children are now grown up, and no longer need her as they once did, there are many specific problems that may come to light in first aid counselling. This situation, in fact, may well provide a ' lead in ' to a number of associated problems which can be greatly helped by effective counselling.

As it presents itself to the counsellor the problem is an all too common one, a middle-aged woman of about fifty, looking rather anxious and depressed, possibly nervy and strained, who seems a little diffident about asking for help, whether she is seen during the minister's calling or whether she deliberately seeks his help. As in all counselling the first aim of the counsellor is to encourage the person to give an account of the problem as she sees it, and particularly to encourage her to unburden all her feelings about it. He assists her to do this by picking up and responding more to the feelings being expressed than to the facts, which are considered in terms of what they mean to the person.

When the woman overcomes her initial diffidence she will most likely unburden herself in some such manner as this :

I'm feeling that there's nothing much left in my life, I'm no longer needed by anyone now that my children don't need me any more. My husband is immersed in his work and his sporting activities, and I might as well be his housekeeper for all he needs of me. I don't seem of much use to him even as a sexual partner, and it means little enough to me now. I've devoted some of the best years of my life to my children and now that they don't need me as they did there doesn't seem anything much to live for.

COUNSELLOR—Life has become empty for you.

THE MOTHER—Yes, it has, and I'm deeply concerned about it. I suppose it had to come, and perhaps I didn't prepare myself enough for it, but I didn't think I'd be left in quite such a lonely and useless state by my husband and children. I can't understand my daughter ; she and I used to be so close, but now she seems to resent my offers of help, and yet she doesn't seem at all backward in using me when it suits her, as a baby sitter or for some other thing that even a young servant girl could do. And she doesn't mind using me to provide some eggs or other items of food when she finds herself without them. Sometimes I feel that she and her husband are just making a convenience of me. My son is not married and he still lives at home, but I hardly see him. He mostly comes in late for meals and uses the home as little more than a boarding house, and he takes very little responsibility for helping me in any way.

COUNSELLOR—They all just take you for granted, and it makes you feel that you've ceased to be needed for anything important as you used to be needed. And it's hard to take.

THE MOTHER—Yes, that's it exactly. I've talked to my daughter and my son about it, but they don't seem to understand, and now I wish I hadn't mentioned it. I must have failed somewhere in their upbringing to make them so insensitive and ungrateful.

COUNSELLOR—They've disappointed you in all this, and made you wonder whether you've failed in their upbringing. And you sound as if you're rather despairing about the future.

THE MOTHER—I'm afraid I am, and that's why I'm hoping you can help me. I feel I'm getting more and more withdrawn into my shell, more and more stodgy and unattractive, and I don't seem to have the energy and enthusiasm I once had, to shake myself out of it. I just feel I'm a wet blanket with everybody, and then I get annoyed with people when I think they aren't interested in me. I know I shouldn't get annoyed, because I bring a lot of it on myself. Yet I can't seem to work up enough energy to make the effort necessary to make friends with anybody.

COUNSELLOR—You feel lonely, and you want friends, but somehow you've been finding it too difficult to raise enough energy to attract them. And you tell yourself that you've lost your attractiveness.

THE MOTHER—If only my husband could understand what I'm feeling, and give me some real encouragement, it might be better. When I tell him how I'm feeling he just says I have no reason to feel like that. He assures me that I'm as good a person as I always was, and that he thinks the world of me. But I *do* feel like that, and I can't seem to get it across to him that I do. He was never able to understand things like that, only things that he can handle and manipulate. Nobody seems able to understand, and I feel terribly alone.

COUNSELLOR—You're fighting a very lonely battle. Well, now that you've been able to tell me about it perhaps we can put our heads together and look a bit more deeply into all that you're facing and then it might not be quite such a lonely one from now on.

THE MOTHER—No, I don't think it will be so difficult. I feel quite a lot better for having talked with you like this. It's the first time I've been able to get it all off my chest, and it's the first time too that anyone has appeared to be at all interested in how I feel. I hope you can help me to find some way out of this ' wet blanket ' kind of misery.

This, in necessarily abbreviated form, may be taken as an example of the possible opening of an initial interview. It illustrates something of the manner in which the counsellor picks out and responds to the feelings rather than the facts communicated to him. It can also illustrate how such responses encourage the unburdening of more feelings, and the development of ' rapport ' between the two people. This will greatly facilitate the further stages in the counselling, which will include the clarification of the whole situation and then the gradual discernment of possible ways of dealing with it.

So far in this woman's narrative we have an account of her intense feelings of defeat, depression, devaluation, and despair, together with her anxiety and apprehensiveness about the bleak-looking future. We also have her sense of past failure and present uselessness, her lack of communication with her husband personally and sexually, and her implied hostility against her daughter and son for their insensitivity and ingratitude, and their way of making use of her. Nothing has so far come into the discussion concerning her health—she is probably going through the change of life (at fifty) and this may well be an important factor in the trouble, and one which some appropriate medical treatment might overcome to a great extent. The counsellor will keep this in mind, and ask her at some appropriate point whether she has seen her doctor recently.

During the ' clarification ' stage of the counselling the counsellor may take up any of the mother's remarks and invite her to discuss the matter more deeply. For example he might guide the discussion along some such line as this :

COUNSELLOR—You mentioned a moment ago that you must have failed somewhere in your children's upbringing. I wonder if you could tell me a little more about that.

THE MOTHER—Well, you see, when the children came my husband was very deeply involved in his work. He had to be, or we wouldn't have had enough money to be able to give them a decent home and proper care and education. I've been thinking a lot about that period of our lives, and I think now that in my loneliness I rather looked too much to the children to meet my needs for companionship. Actually they both had a number of illnesses and I found it difficult to develop many social contacts, especially with my husband so busy and preoccupied. Looking back I think I probably clung to them too much, I had all my eggs in one—or really two—baskets. I used them as a compensation for the emptiness of my marriage, and I don't think I made enough real effort to achieve any real closeness to my husband. I don't think he made much effort either, so perhaps we're both to some extent responsible. Now the children have become independent there's nothing left. But that doesn't excuse my daughter from rejecting my offers of help.

COUNSELLOR—Could it be that your daughter—and possibly your son too—have been a bit rebellious against what may have appeared to them as your need to possess them and to depend too much on them ? Could they have been frightened that you might still want to keep too tight a control over them?

THE MOTHER—I hadn't thought of it in quite that way ; it's hard to put yourself in someone else's place. Yes, that seems to make sense. I wonder if that is what they've been feeling. I certainly hadn't intended it that way.

Counsellor—Would it help if you picked your time and had a quiet talk with them along these lines, and showed them that you're interested in how they've been feeling about you ? Could you take it if they were fairly critical ?

The Mother—It wouldn't be easy—but I think I'd like to try. Do you know, this is the first ray of daylight I've had for quite a time ?

Counsellor—That's fine. You were also concerned about your inability to get across to your husband, to feel at one with him personally and sexually. While we're looking at the family could we look for a moment at that ?

In such a manner as this, again necessarily curtailed, the counsellor may achieve the ' lead in ' to associated problems, which are all important to the presenting one. Any of these can then be picked up and further discussed in later interviews.

With regard to the marital relationship, many important matters influencing both husband and wife may come up for discussion, with improvement in mutual understanding and companionship. As their marriage lost vitality each of them would seem to have compensated for it in different ways. The wife fulfilled her ' need to feel needed ' through caring for the children, and the husband fulfilled his by greater and greater involvement in his work ; and they drifted further and further apart.

A common characteristic of such ' compensatory ' devices is that people tend to over-compensate. The wife did so by becoming rather too possessive, too dependent on the children's dependence on her. The husband probably became more dependent than necessary on his work as a way of feeling needed and important. Other kinds of compensation may be chosen by different people. Husbands may become over-involved in social or sporting activities, with alcohol or with another woman. Wives may over-commit themselves to social or religious activities. Husbands or wives may find escape in sickness, mostly of a neurotic kind, or in separation or divorce.

As often happens this woman is suffering greatly at the very time when, because of the coming of her change of life and the departure of her children, she needs her husband's companionship and help more than at any other time in her marriage. At the same time her husband has become so fixed in his habitual way of life that he finds it difficult to understand, and even more to help.

This is a time at which people generally need to be ready to change direction in order to meet entirely new challenges. Such changes may be difficult, because the present way of life has become habitual, and also because there is also a compulsive element in the compensatory devices, which are felt necessary to preserve status, power, and other props of psychic security. People find it difficult to face and to question these devices unless there is a serious threat to their psychic security. In the present case the mother is threatened to a greater extent than her husband, and for him to come to any real recognition of his wife's needs and his own involvement in her health and welfare, prolonged and skilful counselling may be needed.

In most, if not all cases, the first aid counselling will need to move beyond whatever clarification may be possible to some consideration of what may need to be done or planned as a positive approach to the relief of the woman's distress. This time of change in a person's life needs to be seen as one of challenge. The decision must be made, whether to accept the challenge to new adventures in living, with any temporary professional assistance, or to settle for dreary resignation to a devitalized existence, with all the possibilities of lapsing into a depressive illness, or into separation or divorce.

The counsellor will constantly be asking himself whether the person in front of him is willing or able to take reasonable responsibility for the promotion of her own future welfare, or whether she is assuming that she can or should depend on her husband and her children to solve her problem. He will need to attempt an assessment of the extent to which she may be ' externalizing ' problems that may be largely within herself. He will best do this

68

if he is constantly alert to her responses to his attempts to encourage her to make her own decisions.

Here is where some of the counsellor's religious faith may be able to give some inspiration to the troubled person. This will come more from his general attitude of interest and acceptance and his positive approach, than it will from any attempt to ' preach ' to her. The counsellor will need to be attentive to his own philosophy in all his work, because the person will ' catch on ' to it whether he expresses it verbally or not. He needs to radiate a genuine and well-founded spirit of hope and trust, and possibly to cultivate something of the attitude well expressed by Thomas Carlyle in one of his essays :

> Today is not yesterday : we ourselves change ; how can our Works and Thoughts, if they are always to be the fittest, continue always the same ? Change, indeed, is painful ; yet ever needful ; and if memory have its force and worth, so also has Hope.

Among the positive plans that may well come up for this woman's consideration are those concerning her health, for which medical help may well be most important ; and her appearance, also most important for her morale. Attention to any overweight or ungainliness, to any deficiencies in her skin or her complexion, a new hair-do and some improvement in her dressing could work wonders for a woman who in her general depression may have tended to neglect herself to some extent. Such efforts will help greatly in her efforts to cultivate better personal relationships with her husband, her children, and her friends, and also in any efforts she may be ready to make to open up wider relationships in practical projects.

Many practical projects may well come up for discussion, and for the sake of clarity these may be considered under the four general headings of remunerative work, further study or training, social service, and recreational activities.

How does she feel about seeking, or preparing

for a full time or a part time job ? She may think of this partly as a way of gaining more money for the present or for the future, and partly as a valuable way of finding continued interest and a constructive way of meeting her need to feel needed. Financially it may enable her and her husband to live a fuller and more interesting life after his retirement, and possibly to travel in a way otherwise impossible. In any discussion of this, and other kinds of activity, she will need to guard against any tendency to overdo it and to bring on undue fatigue. She has a need to feel needed which has previously led to some over-compensation for her loneliness, and may need to learn from this previous experience. Any job will of course depend on her ability, health, energy and time, and the availability of jobs which are intrinsically reasonably satisfying.

Apart from salaried jobs she might consider some kind of ' free lance ' occupation, such as writing articles, scripts for broadcasting, plays, books, or poetry. Or she might find it of value to take up a business of her own, a gift shop, or a frock shop or other similar kind. Or she might become available for secretarial work at home, or for child minding or baby sitting. The list is quite a wide one, and if she has or can develop reasonable initiative and patience it is likely that she will find a satisfying occupation of this kind.

Further study or training may be undertaken as a preparation for a new job, or a ' brushing up ' of some previous training, or it may be undertaken for its own interest or for better social service. Such further study may be academic, cultural, or technical.

Academic study may be in subjects at a University, or through some Adult Education service, or in Home Study with the assistance of libraries, magazines, wireless or television programmes, public lectures or study groups, including Bible Study and possibly comparative religion.

At the cultural level (in its widest sense) the study and training available offer a very wide choice. Music, art, literature, drama, astronomy, public speaking, teaching, politics from municipal to national, and international relationships, and many other pursuits can provide great interest to anyone who is temperamentally and intellectually suitable for them, and at the same time bring great improvement in the quality of citizenship.

At the technical level, apart from any training or ' brushing up ' in preparation for a future job, there is a wide choice of all kinds of craft work, and there must be few if any people who could not find some real interest in at least one or two of them. The idea of change may come into the discussion here if the person maintains that she has not previously been interested in any of them. This is the time when a person is challenged to cultivate some new interests, and such cultivation may need some patience and persistence. She might well ask herself, not so much whether she has been sufficiently interested, but whether a particular possibility might be open to the deliberate cultivation of interest in it, and in the opportunities for new friendships it might bring with it.

The third group of practical projects for consideration includes the many kinds of voluntary social service, including church work. Here again there is a very wide choice and the needs are great. The minister will generally have many possibilities to suggest, and there are many more. There are ' solitary ' activities, such as writing braille for the blind, correspondence with lonely or sick people, sewing and mending, and even toy making. More immediately social services include visiting at hospitals, working in auxiliaries or ' opportunity shops ', or in old people's clubs. Every area has its own opportunities, and there are many ways of finding out the main needs in any community which could be met by the devoted service of a person or a group of people.

The fourth group of practical projects includes the recreational activities, those connected with sport, hobbies, and other similar personal interests. There is no reason why the participation in any of these should prevent reasonable participation in activities included in the other three groups. The sporting activities in particular may provide valuable exercise and promote good health as well as enjoyable social relationships. Here again the list is too large to cover in the present discussion.

In the consideration of which activity might be taken up by this woman the possible interests of her husband may be important. Even if she cultivates a number of interests in which it is unlikely that he can share, it is important that she should look carefully at any in which he might have or be able to develop some participation.

In all planning it may need to be remembered that this woman, assuming reasonable health, may have some twenty five or more years of reasonably useful life ahead of her. Fifteen years of this may be with her husband still involved in his work to a greater or less extent, and the remainder with whatever years he may have to enjoy in his retirement. It is worth a lot of care and consideration to find the best way of using this very important part of her life and of enjoying her children in their marriages and her grandchildren in their growth and development. If she can cultivate a non-possessive interest in them all, with acceptance of their different attitudes and different ways, her life will be greatly enriched by them, as long as she can make something worthwhile of it on her own initiative.

We have considered this woman's own feelings about herself and her husband and family, her relationships with them and with the community, and her attitudes to the future and her possible activities. In this we have assumed that her husband is alive and not separated from her. There are many other possibilities, which would need appropriate consideration, but on similar lines to what has been discussed already. If she can rise to the challenge of this situation the way may be opened for still further progressive development, personal and social, to a level beyond anything she has experienced so far.

Behind all her responses to the challenge of this kind of situation there is the need for the achievement of a sense of meaning and purpose which will underpin and sustain all her efforts. If the counsellor has such a sense of meaning and purpose himself and handles his counselling well he may ' infect ' her with something of his own faith, hope and love, and thus give her the best antidote to despair.

In some places this discussion may appear, not only to have pointed beyond first aid, which was right for it to do, but also to have gone beyond it. But in this kind of problem even the less experienced counsellor may well find it possible, or even necessary to go beyond first aid into more continued care. As in most of the problems dealt with in this series it is hard to draw any definite line to suit all problems, all troubled people and all ministers. It is hoped that this account will be of practical help to many ministers as they come face to face with mothers in this kind of distressing situation.

Finally we may see in this woman's experience the need and value of prevention, by helping people in the earlier and middle years of marriage and parenthood to keep looking ahead, and to prepare for what will inevitably come to them in the future. If mothers who have a strong need to feel needed can develop ways of satisfying this need that are more lasting than the children's dependence on them, they will be saved from much heartbreak. In addition all married people may be reminded that marriage needs the regular care and attention due to any living organism if the relationship is to be kept alive and fresh. ' Living happily ever after ' is not automatic in real life, only in the fairy tales, and the minister may do great service to his people by regular reminders of this fact of life.

VII. The Deserted Wife, Husband, or Children

BY WILLIAM L. CARRINGTON, M.D.,
MELBOURNE, AUSTRALIA

WHEN a husband or wife leaves the matrimonial home without any immediate intention to return the deserted partner will generally suffer considerable shock and concern. When the help of the minister or counsellor is sought in such a crisis the future destinies of both partners and any children involved may well depend on his handling of the initial interviews with whoever comes for help.

The deserted wife who seeks help may or may not have any idea of her husband's whereabouts or of his future intentions. She may express herself as completely surprised and bewildered at his action, even though she may later admit that he had made previous threats to leave. In many cases it may be quite clear that her husband has gone with the intention of living with another woman, either immediately or after a hoped for divorce from his wife.

The usual stages of an interview with a deserted wife will be :

1. Encouraging the fullest unburdening of feelings,

2. Assisting in the clarification of the situation,

3. Consideration of immediate needs and of what might be planned for the immediate and long term future.

1. *Encouraging the Fullest Unburdening of Feelings.* The deserted wife may have intense, complex and often contradictory feelings about the situation and about her husband, and it is most important that she be given plenty of time and encouragement to express them. The inexperienced counsellor may be strongly tempted to

begin looking for possible causes and possible solutions before these feelings have been sufficiently ventilated. This may lead to frustration and disappointment, because it is difficult or impossible for a deeply distressed person to assess any such problem clearly until the intense feelings have been sufficiently unburdened. This is one of the important psychological insights on which successful counselling and psychotherapy depend.

The counsellor's first contribution in this, as in all personal counselling, is that he should be a good and attentive listener, allowing the narrative to flow with a minimum of interruption, and picking up and responding to the feelings rather than the facts that are expressed.

He will of course be given many factual details, of how this person discovered that her husband had deserted, of the difficulties that she will have in coping with the children, and many other things. These form an essential part of the unburdening, and the counsellor cannot impede their expression. But his main concern at this moment is about what these things mean to her, how she feels about them. For example, if she says, ' I had no idea he was even thinking of leaving me ; if he had any grievance he might have told me about it, instead of going off in this underhand way ', an appropriate response by the counsellor might be, ' It really rocked you, and you can't understand it '. This would encourage further unburdening of feelings, and help in the achievement of ' rapport '.

As the feelings are being expressed the counsellor should be alert to respond to any mixed feelings that may be communicated, such as feelings of love and hate, dependence and independence. He may do this in quite simple terms, for example, ' You love him and want him back, and yet you feel deeply sore about what he has done and the way he did it ', or ' You can't imagine living without him and you will do anything to get him back, but you're not prepared to be pushed around in the way he seems to have imagined he could do '.

In her anxiety and distress the woman may ask the counsellor a direct question, ' What can I do ? '

at the beginning of the interview. The counsellor may need to be careful here, to avoid attempting a premature answer on the one hand, or appearing to brush off the question on the other, with such a negative response as, ' I can't tell you what to do at this stage ', or ' That's for you to decide '. A more appropriate response might be, ' It's pretty urgent that you should know what to do. Perhaps we can get a better idea of this if you can tell me a lot more about it and about your marriage.'

In some cases the minister will have known all members of the family for some time, and he may have a good idea of the possible reasons for the desertion. He may be strongly tempted to confront the deserted wife with any of these, but it is almost always more helpful to give her time, and to try to create the accepting kind of relationship— accepting her rather than anything she may have done—so that she may possibly achieve her own insight in due course. Any reasons for the desertion may well come into the discussion during the second stage, now to be described briefly.

2. *Assisting in the Clarification of the Situation.* When the unburdening seems to be reasonably complete, for the time at least, the counsellor might encourage some discussion about the marriage and about any conflicts and difficulties that may have been experienced by either husband or wife. An open general question is generally best at the beginning, such as, ' Could you tell me something about your marriage ? ' Later questions might be directed to more specific matters, such as the kinds of things they have quarrelled about, how they have handled differences and conflicts, what attention they gave to the marriage relationship itself, and the extent of communication between them. It is important in this to avoid letting the interview become dominated by a series of questions, and these are only mentioned as matters to be kept in the counsellor's mind, to be asked about if it seems warranted. The continual questioning by a counsellor is generally an indication of his own anxiety, and it will tend to discourage the free and spontaneous expression of feelings and attitudes,

especially of those which may be difficult or humiliating for the person to face.

This clarification may demand great patience, sensitivity and tact. Even if the wife can perceive some of the possible reasons for her husband's desertion or the things that led up to it, she may brush them off as unreasonable, as they may well seem to her. In this situation the counsellor may need to spend some time discussing the proposition that people often see things quite differently and assess them from different points of view. This may involve more time and skill than might seem appropriate for ' first aid ' counselling. The most important function of the counsellor here is to create and preserve the kind of relationship that will encourage any person to persist with counselling, and to carry on with any selected person for long enough to allow for adequate help.

One aspect of the clarification that may well come into the first aid counselling is the discussion of how the husband may be feeling about the situation, the consideration of what may have made him decide to leave. When this question can be faced with the wife the counsellor might clarify the situation a little further and sow the seeds of more constructive thinking by asking her whether she thinks a person can help feeling as he does. The counsellor might ask the wife, for example, whether she can help her feelings, even if other people may find it difficult to understand why she feels as she does. Some realistic appreciation of the need to accept other people's feelings even when we can't understand them may prove to be a vital element in the whole project of reconciliation.

3. *Consideration of Immediate Needs and of what might be Planned for the Immediate and Long Term Future.* Before the end of the first interview there should be some consideration of any immediate needs of the deserted wife, and of possible ways in which they might be met. She may also need to be referred for special legal advice about what she should do in the matter, and if the present counsellor is unable or feels incompetent to conduct the further interviews that may be necessary, some

77

consideration will need to be given to referral for these. If referral is regarded as unnecessary a decision may need to be made about inviting the husband for a discussion of his feelings about the future of the marriage, and about further interviews with the wife. Planning for the longer term future will obviously depend on the attitude of the wife to the whole question of working toward reconciliation, and it may be some time before she feels able to make any definite decision about this, contingent as it may be to some extent on her husband's attitudes and conduct. In many cases the main aim of the 'first aid' counselling, apart from giving the necessary relief and support, will be to establish confidence in counselling itself, about which many people still have distorted or vague ideas.

Counselling with the deserted husband will proceed along much the same lines as already described, but there will generally be some special features. The feelings of the husband will be very complex and often contradictory. He may have intense feelings of hostility, coupled with a strong desire to have his wife back. He may be deeply concerned about the children if his wife has taken them with her, and feel considerable worry if she has left them in his care. If there is another man in the case he will have some very intense feelings about him, and the desire to inflict some kind of retaliatory violence on him. Some husbands show deep self-reproach from the beginning, and a readiness to do anything to help in the reconciliation. In some such cases it may be discovered that there had been repeated mental and physical cruelty on his part, and a consistent refusal to seek any expert help. When in the face of this the husband assures the counsellor that he loves his wife dearly, and that he can't live without her it is clear that the problem is a complex one. In many such cases the wife will have left on previous occasions, and returned in response to her husband's heartfelt appeals and promises, only to find that the cruelty breaks out again after a week or two. This 'sado-masochistic' attitude of the husband will generally need quite skilled help, and he will have more motivation for it if his wife is in no hurry to return, or refuses to do so unless she can see a genuine and well-sustained improvement in her husband's attitudes.

A warning needs to be kept in mind here that if the wife says she will not return unless her husband sees a psychiatrist, the results are likely to be disappointing. If he consents to go at all it will generally be against his will, and he may well attend but take no active part in any therapy. He can then go to his wife and say that he has done what she asked, but that the psychiatrist was no good, and it was a bad mistake to expect him to go. It is not the attendance she is really looking for but the improvement, however achieved, and it is much better that any such ' ultimatum ' should be worded in this practical form.

It is likely that the husband will be unable to see many of the factors which combined to make his wife leave him in quite the same way as his wife will have seen them. Even when he can see some of them only too well he may find it very difficult to admit them, or to realize what they may have meant to his wife. These matters will need to be dealt with in the second ' clarification ' stage of the counselling.

As before the second stage may be introduced by an open question or request, such as ' Could you tell me something about what your marriage has been like over the years ? ' This will give the husband an opportunity to offer his own assessment of the relationship, which may well be more revealing than his response to a specific question is likely to be. At some point it will generally be necessary to encourage him to make some assessment of possible reasons why his wife may have decided to leave. If he maintains that he can see no adequate reason for her desertion the counsellor might offer the suggestion that a person is hardly likely to do something as drastic as this without reasons which seem valid to her, even if nobody else can understand why she should have gone. The husband might then be invited to look carefully at any recollections of conflicts between them, and at any complaints his wife may have made, even if at the time he may have regarded them as unwarranted. A further clue might come from discussion of his 'role perceptions and role expectations' of marriage, his ideas of what husbands and wives should contribute to the relationship. If, for example, he maintains that the husband should be the undisputed 'leader' (he might well mean 'boss') in the home, it may point to a possible reason for the desertion if his wife has different concepts of marriage and has reached the point of despair about ever gaining the right to partnership. This clarification may demand great patience, sensitivity, and tact, and it may require much more than 'first aid' counselling.

The third stage of counselling, consideration of immediate needs and of future plans, cannot be ignored, even in first aid counselling. Among immediate needs there may be some concerned with his own ability to look after himself and his home, the question, if he has a rented house, of whether he would be better to seek board and lodging or to keep up the home in hope of his wife's return. He may need some information about the children's schooling and their health and comfort, which may well be obtainable when his wife needs to make contact with him about maintenance of the children. If he has been left with the children he faces a possible problem of having them properly cared for without his having to risk trouble with his job, all the more important now with the prospect of extra expenses. There will be problems too of his access to his children if they are in the custody of his wife, and these can often be dealt with in counselling when the wife is also willing to participate. If not, the matter may need legal help.

An important prelude to further planning is the possibility of his wife's coming by invitation for counselling, either with or separately from him. In most if not all cases of this kind it will be most helpful to have the wife alone at least for one or two sessions, so that she can have the opportunity to speak freely and express her feelings and attitudes. In later counselling, generally beyond ' first aid ' counselling, a number of joint interviews may be necessary so that many contentious and conflicting matters may be worked through, and broken communications restored. The counsellor in any early or continued counselling should resist the temptation to try to urge them to come together. If they do so without being convinced of its feasibility, it may only take one false move or impulsive word to bring disaster again, with much less hope than previously of reconciliation. It is essential that the decision to resume living together should be quite free and spontaneous for both husband and wife, and it is worth all the extra time and patience that may be needed to allow this to happen. The counsellor can have no ' vested interest ' in their coming together except in this way, however dedicated he may be to the concept of the sanctity of marriage and the welfare of the children.

As before questions of referral for legal advice or for further counselling will generally need to be discussed, and before the termination of any interview the counsellor should make a brief summary of what has been clarified and what has been planned. One further matter about which it may be necessary for the counsellor to give some direct advice is in his future communications with his wife. In his distress and loneliness he may be strongly tempted to keep on pestering her (that is how she may see it) to return to him. This may only convince her that he still wishes to control or manipulate her in his own interests, and to deny her the right of self determination, an essential element of our democratic heritage. It may be helpful for the counsellor to suggest that his wife knows quite well that he wants her back, but that she will be more impressed by any efforts on his part to win back her broken trust, and to respect her freedom to decide for herself in this important matter. He will need to realize that if her trust in him has been broken by his actions he cannot expect to rebuild it by words ; only by showing trustworthiness in action over a sufficient period. If the husband can see this he is less likely to stand in his own light in his sincere and heartfelt efforts to win his wife back.

When husband and wife are each participating in individual counselling it sometimes happens that the counsellor is asked by one to report on what the other has said, particularly what the other has complained about. However tempting it may be to accede to such a request the counsellor should refrain from doing so. In the first place all such material is strictly confidential, and should be confidential even in relation to the marriage partner unless the counsellor has specific permission or a request to disclose it. But even apart from that any ' tale bearing ' may well involve the counsellor in a difficult situation. For example, if a wife has complained about her husband's cruelty and he has made no reference to it in his counselling sessions, the counsellor may feel disposed to tell him that his wife is concerned about his violence. He will most likely brush this off as completely exaggerated or even without foundation, thus blocking any discussion of it. The counsellor is then in a dilemma. Is he to report the husband's comment back to the wife—and her angry comment then back to the husband—and so on ? In such situations it is generally better to attempt to arrange a joint interview as long as each is willing to participate, and to bring up any such complaints not already settled. Then when the husband attempts to brush off the complaint his wife will take the matter up firmly with him, and out of the to and fro discussion some approximation to the truth will emerge. This is then on the ' agenda ' to be taken up possibly with the husband alone in a subsequent interview, assisted by a simple question, ' What is it that stirs you up in this way ? ' In most cases, however, this would be regarded as something more than ' first aid counselling '.

When the help of a minister or counsellor is sought on behalf of deserted children, apart from the desertion of only one parent, the first consideration will almost always be their immediate needs. Whether the parents have actually deserted, or whether they have been prevented from carrying out their responsibilities by death, by accident or severe illness, or by any other catastrophe, the dependent children will need proper accommodation and care. It may be that they still have their place of living, and possibly one or more older children may be able to take some responsibility. In such cases, if the help of suitable relatives cannot be obtained, it may need little more than some regular neighbourly attention from someone living nearby or from a devoted member of the minister's congregation. In other cases, where the children are homeless, or when they are all very young, emergency accommodation will need to be found until suitable arrangements can be made for longer term care. All civilized communities have provision for the care of deserted children, but it is not always easy to arrange such accommodation at very short notice. Fortunately kind hearted neighbours and friends are nearly always very willing to give the kind of emergency relief that is needed.

The actual counselling that may be needed in such cases will generally be given to the children together, possibly with someone who may have them in temporary or permanent care. The immediate counselling need is generally for the opportunity to ' sob it out ', to unburden the confused and distressed feelings of grief, anxiety, hostility and bewilderment. Children, being dependent, will need much more direct comforting and reassuring than adults will need, and the counsellor's own experience of parenthood may be very helpful in this. Above all the children will need the assurance that they will be looked after and cared for by people who will love them, and who will understand their feelings.

The further stages of counselling will be along lines already discussed, but there will be less opportunity for clarification than with adults. The main clarification needed may be of their conflicting feelings, their bewilderment about the circumstances of the 'desertion', and their attitudes to their parents and any other significant people in the situation.

In the 'planning' stage, necessarily dominated by very practical considerations, it is important to give any child old enough to have a point of view the opportunity and encouragement to express it fully. It may be that the wishes of the children are impracticable and cannot be met, but whatever has to be done will be given more co-operation by children who have been given this opportunity and whose feelings have been listened to, accepted, and well considered. The reasons for any less acceptable decisions will generally be given to them, but in addition they need to feel that they are being treated as persons, and valued as such.

In all the planning the personal as well as the physical needs of the children need the most careful consideration. Many people who would agree that 'man does not live by bread alone' still seem to imagine that this does not apply to children. Fortunately in our day the personal needs of orphaned or deserted children are very much more widely realized than in earlier years. In such crises as those we have considered children have a much greater need for mature demonstrative affection of the parental kind than at almost any other time, and above all this affection should be offered 'without strings', without expectation of any particular immediate response. In their bewilderment and distress, and possibly their distrust of every one, they may be literally unable to offer any love or gratitude in return, at least for some time. Those who may accept the responsibility of caring for deserted children may need to be helped to understand this, so that they will not feel that such lack of response is necessarily a reflection on their own loving care, and so that they will not accuse the children of ingratitude.

It is obvious that devoted and wisely administered counselling help in the distressing crises of desertion can be of incalculable value in and far beyond the immediate ' first aid ' situation. Such tragedies, distressing as they are, provide a great opportunity for very practical Christian service, open to ministers and laymen—and lay women—alike.

VIII. The Care of the Aged

(Some notes for Ministers regarding mental disorders)

BY DR. ANTHONY BASHFORD,
THE CLINICAL THEOLOGY CENTRE, NOTTINGHAM

Mental Disorders in the Aged

' The thing I'm afraid of is growing old. I hate that. You get old and you've missed it somehow. The old always resent the young and vice versa ' (John Lennon [1]).

> *An aged man is but a paltry thing,*
> *A tattered coat upon a stick*, unless
> Soul clap its hands and sing, and louder sing
> For every tatter in its mortal dress . . .
>
> Consume my heart away ; sick with desire
> And fastened to a dying animal
> It knows not what it is ; and gather me
> Into the artifice of eternity . . .
>
> (W. B. Yeats [2])

A Few Facts

It is reported that there are now nearly three times as many folk aged sixty and over in the U.K. as there were fifty years ago, and with regard to mental disorder, there is a marked increase in incidence with advancing age. The total population of mental hospitals in England and Wales was 46,308 in 1955 ; one-third of these were over the age of sixty-five, in wards for the old and infirm. Mental hospitals are increasingly becoming old people's homes for the mentally ill (*Supplement on Mental Health*, a statistical review for 1960), and suicide rates reach a peak in most

[1] Braun, Michael, *Love Me Do : The Beatles' Progress* (Penguin Books, 1964), 15.

[2] Yeats, W. B., *Selected Poetry* (Macmillan, 1962), 104.

countries between the sixth and eighth decades (Martin Roth [1]).

The Social Aspects of Mental Disorder in Old Age

Three factors are important.

1. Isolation.
2. Infirmity.
3. Retirement.

1. *Isolation.* According to the Guillebaud report, over two-thirds of the beds in mental hospitals occupied by folk over sixty-five were taken up by the *single*, the *widowed*, or the *divorced*. Evidently it is ' not good for man to be alone '. Loneliness tends to come more to the surface of consciousness as one grows older, and loses relatives and friends by death, though some people have been aware of their essential aloneness from a very early age.

It is often thought, and said, that the reason for the greater aloneness of old folk to-day and for their increasing proportion of admissions to mental hospitals, is the lack of family cohesion and concern. In particular, the charge is made indicting the young for no longer caring for the old. A similar charge was made by Esquirol—but that was in the year 1838. Also, a recent study by Townsend, in Bethnal Green, 1957, has shown that a large proportion of old folk are in close contact with their families, and are in fact both helpful to, and cared for by, the young.

Some of us seem to prefer aloneness, some need constant company ; we need both to be able to exist alone, and in relationship with others.

2. *Infirmity.* The relief of this is largely a medical problem ; but it is useful to all helpers to know the common physical disabilities that frequently aggravate or accompany mental distress in the old. They are : deafness, failing sight, restriction of mobility, cardio-vascular disorders, chronic bronchitis, and chronic joint conditions.

[1] Mayer-Gross, Slater and Roth, *Clinical Psychiatry* (Cassell 2nd. ed. 1960), 477.

It is important to remember the interplay of body, mind, and emotions, and to realize how frustrating the loss of a sense or faculty can be to any of us, and especially to anyone with marked obsessional and perfectionist traits.

Howard Root has suggested that we should look to the creative artist for ' faithful, stimulating, profound accounts of what it is to be alive in the twentieth century ' (Howard Root [1]). If we do, we will often find a preoccupation with age and dying. T. S. Eliot, in *Little Gidding*, has a disturbing but revealing description of what may lie ahead for us ; it could be a salutary reminder, when one becomes irritated by older folk :

> Let me disclose the gifts reserved for age
> To set a crown upon your lifetime's effort
> *First, the cold friction of expiring sense*
> Without enchantment, offering no promise
> > But bitter tastelessness of shadow fruit
> > As body and soul begin to fall asunder.
> *Second, the conscious impotence of rage*
> > At human folly, and the laceration
> > Of laughter at what ceases to amuse.
> And *last, the rending pain of re-enactment*
> > Of all that you have done, and been ; the shame
> > Of motives late revealed, and the awareness
> Of things ill done and done to others' harm
> > Which once you took for exercise of virtue.
> > Then fools' approval stings, and honour stains,
> From wrong to wrong the exasperated spirit
> > Proceeds, *unless restored by that refining fire*
> > Where you must move in measure, like a dancer . . . [2]

There are, however, other possibilities for old age ; and the greatest theologian of this century, Karl Barth, in his eighth decade, wrote the following :

> It is a notorious fact that I have become an old man, and to-day we have a science called gerontology which deals with what can be expected of the old

---

[1] Root, Howard, in *Soundings*, ed. by Alec Vidler (Cambridge Univ. Press, 1962), 18.

[2] Eliot, T. S., *Four Quartets* (Faber & Faber, 1944), 39–40.

man. It is of course many years since I rode horse-back through field and wood or performed modest soldierly duties. Climbing uphill no longer tempts me. And even my work pace at the desk has become perceptibly slower. But *in view of the troubles of so many other old people I am thankful for undeserved blessings* : I am not beset by any illness of which I am conscious ; air, water, substantial nourishment and moderate exercise still help me to keep my vigour ; and even my faithful pipe still agrees rather well with me and is not prohibited by my wise physician . . .[1]

3. *Retirement.* Frequently a man's whole life has been centred around his work ; he will even at times spend most of his waking hours believing and stating that he is ' working for the family '. In actual fact, he may be using the work to give himself a reason for living, and when it comes to an end, so does his enjoyment, his initiative, his sense of purpose and usefulness. He finds that the family for whose benefit he has ostensibly been striving, he cannot bear to live with ; he gets more and more resentful, frustrated, embittered, be-comes depressed, and ends up by taking his own life. One later hears the plaintive cry of the bereaved widow—' And after all these years he'd worked—surely he deserved a bit of rest and enjoyment ? '.

The hazards and unexplained malignities of life take a heavy toll in later years ; cancer appears, and pain and grief ensue. There is no answer, no explanation ; the ' dark line ' on God's face remains, and no word is forthcoming as yet. Obviously, the one certainty we have in this life is death ; and the cynic has rightly said, ' Life is a malignant disease, with a very bad prognosis '.

And yet—' *If in this life only we have hope in Christ, we are of all men most miserable* '—St. Paul is invariably relevant, especially to-day when

[1] Barth, Karl, in *How My Mind has Changed*, ed. by Fey, Harold E. (Meridian Books, World Pub. Co., 1961), 25–26.

many still think of Christianity in terms of a vague immortality of the soul, instead of the radical resurrection of the body, which is a far more shattering and yet hope-inspiring fact.

There are times when one longs to hear again the majestic fullness and glory of the gospel of the grace of God. Do we need to return again to the old way ? If we do not believe, may it be in part that the ' foolishness of the thing preached ' has ceased to be sounded as it once was ? If folk have little or no valid faith, is it necessary to return in the assurance of the Holy Spirit's activity to the fundamental facts of the life and death and resurrection of our Lord ? For it is this alone, as P. T. Forsyth phrases it, that *creates belief in itself*. *It pleased God, by the foolishness of preaching, to save them that believe.*

Then let it be the whole gospel itself that is spoken, in all its almighty range and depth, not ' spiritual uplift ' or one's personal experience of the ' absence of God ', or last-minute coaching in morality for those approaching their finals.

Perhaps we have not yet entered into the fullness of our inheritance in Christ ; and the fear of death, perhaps the most persistent of all, will crop out more frequently as we grow older, though it may reveal itself in a variety of ways. And in dealing with the elderly, the minister must be sure of his own strong faith, because it is a distressing field of action, needing much patience, and no blinking of the facts—and some of them are pretty grim.

Mental Disease in Old Age

' The prognosis of mental disorders in old age is probably better than one would anticipate . . . the psychiatrist of today knows that many old people recover or improve even following psychotic breakdown ' (Martin Roth [1]).

It is all too common to assume that anyone of advancing years is necessarily ' going senile ', or ' soft in the brain ', yet it is possible to distinguish

[1] *Clinical Psychiatry*, as above, 505.

five main groups of mental disease of the old. An awareness of this will be valuable to ministers in hospital visitation, and also with regard to the future outlook.

The Five Common Disorders

1. *Affective Illness.* Depression accounts for 90 per cent. or more of these ; the remaining 5–10 per cent. are those of mania or hypomania.

(a) *Depression.* It is sometimes useful to remember the prevalence of the three ' A's '— Anxiety, Agitation, Apathy—noting that *anxiety*, restlessness, and, at times, extreme *agitation* may often be found together, but sometimes *apathy* is marked, *agitation* absent, and *anxiety* is much less apparent.

Common accompaniments are sleeplessness, loss of appetite, marked gloom, a sense of hopelessness, constipation, and ideas of guilt, bodily pre-occupation and/or delusions (*e.g.*, bowels rotting away ; self utterly bad and contaminating neighbourhood).

The risk of suicide is high and admission to hospital is frequently urgently required, and may be initially life-saving ; at the same time, there is no doubt that many old folk can be helped through some depressions if seen early enough, and steadily and patiently, by ministers who are aware of their problems and the resources available to them in Christ, in His word, His Sacraments, His community, above all His acceptance and forgiveness.

Remember the prevalence of ' the root of rage ', and also how often in the old this is linked with present circumstances, with neglect, with loss of loved ones, with ever-increasing frustration over failing senses and abilities. The rage of the old can be extremely violent, as W. B. Yeats has shown.

What shall I do with this absurdity—
O heart, O troubled heart—this caricature,
Decrepit age that has been tied to me
As to a dog's tail ?

> Did all old men and women, rich and poor,
> Who trod upon these rocks or passed this door,
> Whether *in public or in secret rage*
> *As I do now against old age* ?

No, not all ; but a great many do ; and therefore we should expect it, and come prepared and well-armed—else we shall soon be fuming with irritation ourselves. A re-reading of *King Lear* may prove more profitable than many a textbook on geriatrics. George Macdonald, who was well qualified by his own life-experience to write of the old, wrote of Lear :

> We find in him an old man with a large heart, hungry for love, and yet not knowing what love is ; an old man as ignorant as a child in all matters of high import ; with a temper so unsubdued, and therefore so unkingly, that he storms because his dinner is not ready by the clock of his hunger ; a child, in short, in everything but his grey hairs and wrinkled face, but his failing, instead of growing strength . . . But . . . let him learn at last that ' love is the only good in the world ' . . . let the generous great old heart swell till it breaks at last—not with rage and hate and vengeance, but with love ; and all is well : it is time the man should go to overtake his daughter ; henceforth to dwell with her in the home of the true, the eternal, the unchangeable . . .[2]

(b) *Mania* is the extreme opposite of depression, characterized by extreme over-activity, flight of ideas, delusions of power, wealth, or grandeur. Although the mood is preferable to the gloom of depression, yet the flood of activities and bizarre ideas are a sore trial to friends and relatives. The patient is blissfully unaware of the real state of things, and may be blithely and lustily singing ' Onward Christian Soldiers ', or proclaiming to all that she is about to give birth to the Messiah, while gaily ordering half a dozen new washing machines and filling in cheques for £1,000 for the ' dear

[1] Yeats, W. B., as above, 105.

[2] Macdonald, George, *A Dish of Orts* (Sampson Low, 1893).

Vicar '. This is usually a case for urgent hospital admission, and the folk who need help from the burden are the relatives. The patient's great need is of in-patient care, and a subsequent guarding against exhaustion ; sustained drug therapy and constant nursing are required.

2. *Senile Disorder*. This is a distressing condition, slow and insidious in onset, and due to atrophy of the brain itself. It is characterized by :

(a) Disintegration of intelligence.

(b) Dulling of emotions.

(c) Diminution of initiative.

Memory is noticeably impaired ; retention and recall of recent events fails, though incidents of long ago remain clear.

Sleep becomes broken, and folk often ' potter ' about the house, carrying out repetitive, apparently aimless, and sometimes inappropriate acts—switching on the wireless, turning lights or gas off and on, visiting neighbours at odd hours, planning impossible journeys by train or bus, for example.

The illness progresses slowly but relentlessly, and within two years the personality may have reached the stage of marked deterioration. Relatives are accused of stealing pathetic possessions, and retreat into early childhood life and events may occur. The sufferer finds it hard to follow the thread of conversation, or logical thought, tires rapidly, and cannot cope with anything new or unfamiliar.

At times abnormal sexual behaviour crops out. Habits deteriorate quickly, and loss of bladder and bowel control is frequent. The ' dignity of old age ' becomes the dependent helplessness of the child, and treatment in hospital with constant supervision may be required. The minister can often do nothing but watch and pray, and relieve the distress and the guilt feelings of the relatives. Temporary improvement can occur from skilled hospital care, and relatives who have in fact reached the end of their tether may be both willing and able to take up their burden again after a spell of rest from the constant stress of looking after a very disturbed parent. (N.B. This is not to be confused with the ordinary failings and hazards of ageing ; it is an illness due to loss of functioning cells of the brain, and, as such, is inevitably progressive and irreversible.)

3. *Arteriosclerotic States*, due to what is commonly called hardening of the arteries.

As in (2) recent memory is an early casualty ; restlessness, night wandering, confusion, and intellectual fluctuation are common. ' Emotional lability ' is often marked—*i.e.* rapid swing of mood, tears being followed by laughter. (The minister should not be unduly disturbed if an old parishioner bursts into tears when he appears ; next day, or even within a few minutes, the picture may well have changed.) Until very late, judgment, personality, and insight often remain intact. The awareness of the failure of abilities is often a cause of distress, and there is a great need for patient, reiterated reassurance from the minister. Also, marked variation and fluctuation of the state occurs, so that a person may seem quite muddled and confused one day, but clear-thinking and rational the next. Roth has a fine description of a central fact of this condition : ' The impression . . . is one of patchy destruction which leaves the general framework of the personality intact.' [1]

Death finally results from cerebral, kidney, or heart failure, or chest infection.

4. *Delirious States.* These are mentioned because they are relatively common and the priest will no doubt meet them. They are characterized by clouding of consciousness. The main treatment is that of the underlying condition, *i.e.*, it is primarily the doctor's province.

The person is disorientated for time and place ; attention is fleeting ; he cannot grasp the situation ; thinking is disconnected ; delusions and hallucinations may be present.

The hospital visitor should know that delirium

[1] *Clinical Psychiatry*, as above, 525.

may sometimes occur temporarily after operations ; one may frequently ' abandon hope ' or be unduly pessimistic if this fact is not realized. (Nevertheless, a delirious state is always a grave complication.)

Fluctuation of awareness, mistaken though rich thought content, variable orientation and recent onset, are characteristic of delirious states.

Diagnosis of the underlying cause, and prompt treatment of it with skilled nursing care, is a matter of urgency in these states.

5. *Late Paraphrenia.* Just as one begins to venture a sigh of relief at having entered the later stages of life without having fallen a prey to the many hazards of life that one has read and heard about, having coped valiantly with one's hysterical tendencies, stormed one's way through a host of depressions, managed to winkle oneself out of bouts of isolation, and come to wry terms with one's peevishness, resigned to the fact that maybe a lot of folk do have good reason to dislike one, just as one dares to hope that a time of rest and peace and quiet is due, one more illness may appear.

In this, the personality is apparently un-impaired, except for the presence of persecutory delusions. It occurs more commonly in women, and also in the unmarried of both sexes. Hearing or sight are affected in about one-third of these patients.

At the time of the onset of illness, the person may become quieter, more solitary and with-drawn. Friends, relatives, neighbours are sus-pected, and police, parsons, bishops, royalty, and the government are bombarded with complaints, verbal or written. The neighbour is accused of trying to obtain the property or the money or the life of the patient. Lights and noises are thought to be signs of the enemy's activities. Poison is pushed through the walls or the pipes. The radio, the television, send death rays or voices that slander or accuse the patient. At times men are thought to be approaching to attack ; strange feelings in the body signify violation by occult

95

means. Sometimes a person feels influenced by another's hypnotic or magical powers, and feels compelled to submit to their outrageous demands.

Memory, reason, concentration, attention are unimpaired. I include reason because, as Chesterton has said, the one thing a lunatic has not lost is his reason. Do not attempt rational discussion or dissuasion with regard to the delusions. You will invariably lose the argument, the possibility of helping the patient—and your own temper !

When disturbance is marked, and hospital admission necessary, treatment may provide temporary, and at times even lasting, relief ; but as yet there is no known cure. We need to learn much more. One of the hardest and often most unrewarding tasks is the attempt simply to make friends with one of these sufferers ; yet it may be the way which will ultimately prove of greatest value.

These outlines of the major mental disorders of older folk are brief and inadequate : but they may prove of value, if only to point to the differing conditions, and perhaps to cast a faint light in some dark places. The ' treatment ' is always ultimately that of the person ; but every insight into causation and awareness of symptom grouping can be helpful, if not always to the sufferer, certainly to the helper.

It may be useful to summarize the positive attitudes which have been recommended to counsellors in the course of the article :

(1) To aim to alleviate loneliness without invading treasured privacy.

(2) To remember the ' root of anger ' in age and the frustration caused by increasing infirmities.

(3) To remember that retirement may deprive some people of the whole sense of purpose in living.

(4) To give proper place to ' love ', both in those giving counsel and those receiving it.

(5) The need to treat the *whole* person rather than individual symptoms.

(6) To offer the Gospel in its *fullness* (with an emphasis on the Christian's hope, both here and now, and beyond death).

(7) To emphasize the adequacy of resources available in Christ, the Word, the Sacraments, the community and forgiveness.

(8) The need for the minister himself to have ' the full assurance of faith ' in his contacts with old people.

The teacher to whom I owe most, Oswald Chambers, constantly expounded these great truths of the Faith. His talks on Ecclesiastes [1] are extremely relevant to-day and, in conclusion, I know nothing better than his words on Redemption :

> We can never expound the Redemption, but we must have strong unshaken faith in it so that we are not swept off our feet by actual things. Everything that has been touched by sin and the devil has been redeemed ; we are to live in the world immovably banked in that faith. Unless we have faith in the Redemption, all our activities are fussy impertinences which tell God He is doing nothing . . . if we say we believe ' It is finished ' we must not blaspheme God by unbelief in any domain of our practical life.[2]

---

[1] Chambers, Oswald, *Shade of His Hand* (Oswald Chambers Pubs. Assn. and Marshall, Morgan & Scott, 1961).

[2] Chambers, Oswald, *Thy Great Redemption* (Oswald Chambers Pubs. Assn. 1958), 11.

IX. Christian Ministry to the Dying

By Canon Sydney Evans,
Dean of King's College London

It is with great hesitation that I take up my pen
to write about death and Christian ministry to one
who is dying. I have accepted the invitation to
attempt this article not from such resources of
experience of being with dying persons as belong
to a hospital chaplain or parish priest ; my
personal experience of being with dying persons is
very limited. I agreed to do this prompted rather
by the realization of my ignorance and inexperience
and therefore of my need to clarify my mind and
prepare myself for a ministry which I may as a
man and a priest be called on to exercise at any
moment. I have read some of the books and
articles that have been written by those who have
the right to share experience and reflection on that
experience ; I have talked with doctors and with
clergy whose work has brought them frequently
into touch with the actuality of dying. Those who
have read articles by or have heard lectures from
Dr. Cicely Saunders [1] and the Reverend Norman
Autton [2] will recognize the indebtedness of this
article to them.

Sweeping generalizations will be out of place in
such an area of human experience as the one we
are considering. Everyone must die. But each
person dies his or her own death. Both the actual
circumstances of dying and the attitude to the
onset of death will be unique to each individual
person. However often we are in the presence of
dying persons we have never before been in the
presence of this particular person and his dying.

For some, death is sudden and unexpected. For
others, there will be illness of longer or shorter

[1] *E.g.*, reprint from the *Nursing Times*, 26th November, 1965—' Watch with Me '.

[2] *Death and Bereavement* (Christian Knowledge
Booklets, S.P.C.K., 1965) ; *The Pastoral Care of the
Dying* (S.P.C.K., 1966).

duration, of greater or less severity. Some will have thought about death in the course of life and will have to some extent come to terms with it. Others will have avoided the thought and be very much afraid. Even if not afraid of death, people often are afraid of actually dying. Because death is at the same time inevitable for all but unpredictable for any, Christian ministry to the dying must needs begin as a ministry to the living. The way in which a person lives will make a difference to the way in which he dies. Jeremy Taylor reminds us that the best preparation for holy dying is holy living. And Richard Baxter tells that we are ' to preach as never sure to preach again, as a dying man to dying men '. ' In the midst of life we are in death.'

If we have been brought up within the worshipping community we shall all our lives be familiar with death ; if not with the actuality of dying, certainly with the fact of death and with an attitude towards the fact that is secretly and deeply being built up within us. The crucifixion of Jesus, baptism into His death and resurrection, regular participation in the action of the eucharist, the learning how in daily relationships to ' die ' to selfishness and to ' rise again ' into outgoing love, the whole Christian understanding of discipleship as a dying to live, all these little deaths we voluntarily die to self are rehearsals for that greater death when we must hand ourselves over finally to the God to whom we have been learning to hand ourselves over all our lives. To live the Christian life in this world is already to live in some degree beyond death in a faith relationship to Him who is alive for us beyond His own death. The whole liturgical, theological, moral, and spiritual atmosphere of life in the Christian community is a preparation for death, and death for the Christian is to be thought of as a transition from one relationship with God to another. Of this relationship with God beyond death we know nothing. Our confidence is in the character of God as He has made Himself known in Christ crucified and risen.

But we cannot assume a similar experience in

any but a minority of the dying persons with whom we shall come into contact as nurses or as doctors or as priests.

Two preparations are necessary for those who are to serve men and women who must die. First, they must work out a theology of death ; secondly, they must face the fact and come to terms with the fact that they too will die. There needs to be a background of intellectual, psychological, and spiritual preparation for pastoral work. This is as necessary for the nurse as for the priest. And a large part of the ordained minister's ministry to the dying will be in relation to those who as doctors and nurses and friends will be in more continual contact with the dying than he will himself. How he will be of service to these other servants of the dying will depend on circumstances. But his ability to be of service to them will depend on his own preparedness and his ability to establish a relationship of trust and confidence with these others. There is need of mutual trust between all who are ministering to the patient : doctor, priest, nurse, social worker must work together as a team.

A theology of death for to-day will need to take account of the Christian tradition and of modern biblical and doctrinal criticism of that tradition ; it will need no less to take account of modern medical knowledge and of contemporary attitudes.

Geoffrey Gorer's *Death, Grief and Mourning in Contemporary Britain* [1] is one source of information about contemporary attitudes. The minister should read also Evelyn Waugh's *The Loved One* and Jessica Mitford's *The American Way of Death* so that he may know the extremes to which some will go in pretence that death is not a reality. Pascal, as so often, put his finger on a human trait when he said : ' We spend all our lives trying to take our minds off death '. Few of us would say that we really felt at ease in the presence of a dying person.

In seeking a theology of death the Christian minister must not avoid the harsh realities of dying. There is much to be gained by ordinands serving for a time as hospital orderlies. The

[1] Cresset Press, 1965.

Christian must face not only the physical distress and humiliation that sometimes accompany terminal illness but also the mental agony, the tearing of human affection and relationships.[1] Reality must not be covered over with sentimentality. 'Death is an outrage', so Charles Williams, a lay theologian, once began a course of lectures on the Passion of Jesus. A very different person, Simone de Beauvoir, writing about her mother's death,[2] reaches the conclusion : 'There is no such thing as a natural death : nothing that happens to a man is ever natural, since his presence calls the world in question. All men must die : but for every man his death is an accident and even if he knows it and consents to it, an unjustifiable violation.' I believe she is right and we shall be less than Christian if we cannot be human enough to feel death as an 'outrage' and an 'unjustifiable violation'. The crucifixion of Jesus is both. Biblical writers often speak of death as the enemy and the intruder. It is only when we allow this to be faced that we shall appreciate the glory of a Gospel that redeems even death. Oliver Quick (*Doctrines of the Creed*, 210 ff.) analyses this and concludes : 'thus it is that Christianity, alone among the religions and philosophies of the world, succeeds in eliciting from death, *i.e.*, from the actuality of dying, a unique value, so that it is found to make a positive and necessary contribution to the perfection of created life—to it dying is an essential part or moment in that act through which love accomplishes the self-sacrifice which issues in eternal life. And this physical death, in all its terrible universality, becomes for the Christian a sacrament of the spiritual truth that because it is love which saves, life must be lost before it can be fully won.'

At this point the minister in search of a theology of death might well turn to *Le Milieu Divin* in which Père Teilhard de Chardin writes pene-

[1] N. W. Clerk (C. S. Lewis), *A Grief Observed* (Faber and Faber, 1961).

[2] *A Very Easy Death*, trans. Patrick O'Brien (Weidenfeld and Nicolson, 1966).

tratingly and positively about man in his strength and in his weakness, in his activities and in his passivities, especially in those diminishments of vital powers which come with age.

But if a theology of death is one essential element in the preparing of ourselves to be able to serve the dying, no less important is the formation of our own character and personality. The heart of this ministry to the dying and to those who serve the dying is deeply personal—a relationship of mutual trust to be established between the person who is dying and those who are in touch with him or her, either professionally or as friends. This is an exercise of understanding love.

This kind of love has been defined as ' self-forgetful concentration on the true being of " the other " '. ' Self-forgetfulness ' has to be achieved ; and only when it has been achieved can we be ourselves unembarrassed in the presence of the dying person and so spare him embarrassment. To be unembarrassed means that we have overcome our own fears of death by facing death in ourselves, in others, in Christ ; by accepting death as part of the total mystery of being human ; by discovering that the process of dying is itself a process of closer unity and communion with God. ' Self-forgetfulness ', therefore, would seem to be a by-product of a living faith and love, and these can be ours if we desire them enough and expose ourselves in complete openness to the action of God in our minds and hearts. ' Concentration ' means that—for this period of meeting—this person and myself are all that matter, that our meeting is in the dimension we call God, that I give my undivided attention in courteous respect to this unique person who is going through this unique experience. The ' true being of the other ' is this unique self who is coming to terms with all that is involved in dying. The concentration will express itself in a loving, listening attention, the desire and the effort to understand, concerned not for what *we* shall say to the dying person but for what the dying person will say to us. We shall want with the utmost sensitivity to help the dying person to express his fears and anxieties. Dr. Saunders has written : ' We should face honestly the thought of the anxiety and depression of a long deteriorating illness or the loss of faculties, and the humiliation and deprivation, the guilt aroused by dependence, weakness, incontinence and the sometimes desperate feeling of isolation from life and the living. I once asked a man who knew he was dying what he needed above all to know in those who were caring for him. He said : " For someone to look as if they are trying to understand me ".'

Someone who knew Père Teilhard de Chardin well wrote this about him : ' The look in his eyes when they met your eyes revealed the man's soul : his reassuring sympathy restored your confidence in yourself. Just to speak to him made you feel better : you knew that he was listening to you and that he understood you.' [1] What that person experienced is what we shall want all dying persons to feel about those who minister to them. What the dying ask of us is the true meeting of persons described by Paul Tournier in *The Meaning of Persons* [2] and by Martin Buber in *I and Thou*. ' They need ', writes Dr. Saunders again, ' someone who will come to this meeting not bearing any kind of technique, be it therapeutic, pastoral or evangelistic, but just as another person. A dying man needs practical help given with a compassionate matter-of-factness and simplicity, so that he knows that he is accepted and valued just because he is himself. This can bring the shedding of his physical and mental burden which leave him free at last and greatly eases his response to the things of the spirit.'

A not infrequent difficulty met with in ministering to the dying arises from circumstances in the home or hospital ward where the family or staff attitude is opposed to any genuine preparation for death. The priest will sometimes have to win the trust of relatives and hospital staff if he is to overcome the unreality in relationships with the

[1] Pierre Leroy, *Letters from a Traveller*, 15 (Collins, 1962).

[2] S.C.M., 1957.

dying person which arise from this pretence. Whether in a home or in a hospital ward what matters for the dying is the atmosphere created by all who come in contact—an atmosphere of peace, acceptance, reality, the very opposite of fuss, evasion, and pretence. Wherever possible the minister should try to establish a relationship with the patient before the final stages are reached. Our over-anxious desire to talk, to reassure with a barrage of words, must give place to a loving, listening attentiveness which communicates real caring and will open up the dying person's secret and enable him to speak what is in his heart. Only the patient can reveal to us the degree of his insight into his condition, and what we say to him about his condition must wait upon and be controlled by what he reveals. ' Somewhere within him is the knowledge of the approach of death, although it may never reach the surface of his thought.' Dr. Saunders, out of her many years of close association with dying persons, believes that each person in his or her own time comes to the point when they are ready to put what is for them the key question. She sees it as the work of the persons who watch and serve the dying to wait for that moment and to be relaxed and ready to say what is appropriate in this moment. ' It is the dying who will teach us how to think of them and approach them, if we will only look at their dignity through their dependence and help them to forget all the things they cannot do, and if we will see our own need reflected in theirs and meet them on the same level.'

It is not by words for the most part that we shall communicate a divine reassurance to the dying, but by the quality of our human and Christian presence, by our ' self-forgetful con-centration on the true being of " the other " '. Dying is an utterly lonely experience and the need is for somebody to be there. To hold the dying person's hand can help to overcome their sense of being abandoned or untouchable. Some are helped by being given a crucifix to hold. Words are none the less important, not only for the dying person but for members of the family who are at the bedside. At the end of a pastoral visit a priest will be able to ask quietly and simply : ' May I pray with you before I go ? ' And his prayer will need to be very simple and well known. Few of the dying have a developed faith and life of prayer, but we can never tell what recollections of childhood faith and prayer may come to the surface at the close of life. But the very ill and the untaught cannot manage more than a simple sentence or two and the Lord's prayer with a blessing and a hand placed gently on the forehead. A nun who has worked with dying persons for thirty years uses such prayers as these :

> O my God, I believe in You.
> O my God, I love You.
> O my God, I am sorry for my sins.
> O my God, I offer You my sufferings.
> Jesus, Saviour, I give You my heart.

Such simple prayer will open up the inner soul to receive a real peace. Norman Autton reminds us that the last physical sense to disappear seems to be the hearing. The priest needs to be well prepared with simple, well-known prayers, with biblical texts and perhaps verses of hymns which will greatly help during the final hours people who have themselves become inarticulate. We must say for them some of the things they would like to say for themselves. We must also be on our guard about things we say to others in the presence of a heavily sedated or unconscious person who may well be able to hear without our realizing this.

For those who have lived more committedly within the Christian community there will be desire to receive Holy Communion during terminal illness, and perhaps anointing with oil and the more formal action of laying on of hands.[1] In the case of some at a particular stage in a terminal illness there will be the desire to make confession and receive absolution. These special ministrations of the Church will be suggested and given in

[1] *The Priest's Vade Mecum*, edited T. W. Crafer (S.P.C.K. 1961).

the exercise of such sensitive pastoral concern as I have tried to indicate in this article. Sacraments are not a substitute for personal caring ; they are a particular expression of that caring, the caring of God which it is the purpose of our caring to convey. As one priest has written to me, ' the sacraments are so often the very *means* of personal caring when the resources of caring through normal expressions of love are at a low ebb. I have found that Holy Communion and anointing have been extra-ordinarily effective focal points both for dying people and their relatives, making the whole situation redemptive and reorientating everyone's attitude to death.'

X. The Bereaved

By William L. Carrington, M.D.,
Melbourne, Australia

Some of the most difficult and heart-rending experiences for the Minister are concerned with helping people to work through the crisis of bereavement, the loss of a loved one, husband, wife, child, or parent. Whether or not the loss had been expected and prepared for, the actual event generally comes as a stunning blow, or at least a most distressing emotional experience. Even when the death quite obviously brings merciful liberation from the degeneration and feebleness of extreme old age, or from the ' living death ' of advanced progressive incurable disease, it is still a crucial event in the lives of relatives and friends as earthly ties are broken beyond repair. When in addition the bereavement brings further problems such as deprivation of necessary care and support, it may be felt as an utterly devastating experience, especially in the case of young children.

For the Counsellor, Minister, or layman, suddenly involved in a situation of this kind, possibly charged with the responsibility of breaking the news to the bereaved person, it is necessary, in preparation for this delicate and far-reaching task, to know something of the sequence of reactions which may be expected to occur in grief-stricken people. Although it is outside the strict limits of the present subject it is worth a reminder that comparable reactions tend to occur with almost any other kind of sudden or serious loss, loss of a lover or a friend, loss of job, loss of a limb or of eyesight or hearing, and even sometimes loss of faith.

These reactions have been observed by countless people over the centuries and across the world, and many rituals and ceremonials have come into being to assist people to deal with the inescapable sufferings of bereavement. In recent years ' the grief reaction ' has been studied in greater depth and detail by experts, and their findings have confirmed and added to the wisdom of the ancient rituals.

Each successive stage in the sequence of reactions has its special needs, and if the Counsellor can recognize and understand what is happening he can offer the most valuable help at this critical time in people's lives, not least through his own calmness and confidence. When, on the other hand, the situation is handled inappropriately, great and lasting harm may be done.

The possible stages in the grief reaction, in the order which is commonly experienced, are as follows :

1. Shock.
2. The General Emotional Reaction.
3. Somatic Symptoms.
4. Specific Emotional Reactions.
     Depression, Loneliness, Confusion and
          Helplessness,
     A Sense of Guilt,
     A Sense of Hostility.
5. Idealization of the Beloved.

For present purposes these will be discussed in that order, remembering that the order may vary in different cases and that some of the reactions may not appear in any individual case.

1. *Shock*. The bereaved person may feel stunned, dazed, and overwhelmed at first awareness of what has happened. This initial shock may show itself in various ways. There may be an actual collapse or an inability to believe that the person has really died. The shock may be hidden behind a mask of calm courage and poise, but this is generally a protective mechanism against ' going to pieces ' in front of other people, which still demands considerable courage in the face of the mental agony. This calm exterior may persist with moments or periods of release, right through the funeral arrangements, but if it continues for much longer one may suspect that special help may be needed.

At this stage the Counsellor's best contribution

is to ' be there ', quietly standing by, showing sympathetic acceptance of the bereaved person's feelings, more by a hand on the shoulder than by too many words. As rest is a basic therapy for shock the Counsellor might encourage it as tactfully as possible, for example by quietly taking over and organizing any necessary arrangements, finding out about any further requirements, and possibly protecting the shocked person from some well-meaning but over-intense people.

Words often seem quite inadequate at this time, and if used they should simply express understanding and acceptance of the feelings of shock and bewilderment. It may be tempting to praise the bereaved person's courage, but this is often a two-edged sword, and inappropriate at this stage. Even though the person is courageously struggling to keep a measure of self-control he may not feel particularly courageous at that time. It is even more important to realize that by commending such high standards of courage the Counsellor may unwittingly make the later and essential emotional catharsis appear to the bereaved person as ' cowardice ', or as a ' letting down of standards ', and so make it much more difficult.

While considering words, it may need to be realized that this is an absolutely inappropriate time for attempts at logical reasoning, or the answering of such agonized questions as ' Why did this happen to me ? '. It is much more helpful to respond to such questions by showing simple acceptance of the expressed feeling, such as, ' It's beyond your understanding '. If the initial shock is coupled with intense hostility, for example in the case of parents of a healthy young child run over and killed by a drunken or careless motorist, the most effective response again is one that simply conveys acceptance of the expressed feelings, such as, ' It's overwhelming to you ', or ' You'd like to get your hands on him '. Attempted explanations, justifications, or detailed assurances may well fail to ' get across ' at this stage. For a child who has lost a parent or a sibling the main need at this time is generally the loving physical contact of a calm and sympathetic person with warmth and understanding. Beyond the assurance that he will continue to be loved and cared for, words are generally best left until later.

2. *The General Emotional Reaction.* This may vary considerably in different people and different circumstances between the negative ' freezing up ' and the positive ' sobbing it out '. It is generally agreed that for a constructive and healthy response to grief it is necessary that the person, without too much delay, should allow quite full expression of pent-up feelings, preferably at some time in the presence of at least one acceptable person. The value of such emotional release has been recognized by experience over the ages, and expressed in the music, art, and literature of the world as well as in religious and social rituals. A good literary example is to be found in Shakespeare's *Macbeth*, when Malcolm, on hearing that his wife and babes had been savagely killed, remarks :

Give sorrow words, the grief that does not speak,
Whispers the o'er fraught heart and bids it break.

Modern psychiatric research has confirmed the value of emotional catharsis in this and other circumstances. It has been abundantly demonstrated that those who remain ' frozen up ' in their grief and sorrow almost invariably suffer prolonged and even serious depression.

But emotional release may lose much of its value if it is not handled appropriately. There are two extremes of faulty handling. First there is the over-sympathetic attitude which may promote negative self-pity rather than positive liberation. It may also encourage the person to go on seeking such ' comfort ' rather than to set out on the essential task of rebuilding a self-reliant life. Second, at the other extreme, is the misguided attempt to ' save ' the person from having to go through the emotional release, on the assumption that it may be too distressing. There are many ways of doing this. There may be attempts at ' comfort ' by suggestions that ' You still have a lot to be thankful for ' or that ' Time will heal ', or by the implication that others have had to go through the same or greater suffering. Well-meaning friends can easily try to ' help ' by keeping the person actively occupied or by talking to him about all kinds of things other than the one who has died.

Sometimes a doctor can block the emotional release by yielding too easily to requests for day-time sedation ' to relieve the suffering ', more often made by a relative on behalf of the bereaved than by the bereaved person. The ensuring of a good night's rest by night sedation is a merciful and valuable service, but undue daytime sedation may ultimately do more harm than good when it interferes with the necessary emotional release.

When the bereaved person appears to find difficulty in ' sobbing it out ', the Counsellor (who may be a minister, doctor, relative, or good friend) may help by responding to the person's non-verbal communication by some appropriate remark, such as, ' It still feels quite overwhelming ', or ' You're still feeling lost '. Alternatively, an invitation may be given at some appropriate time to talk about the loved one. Such a remark as ' You must have some wonderful memories of him ', or ' He must have been a very kind man, I'd like to know more about him ', may help to open the door to the necessary release. Invitations of this kind are usually more helpful than the direct suggestion, ' Wouldn't it help to let the tears come ? ' or ' This is a time when you don't have to be brave '.

When the grief does come pouring out, the Counsellor can help best as a rule by just listening and responding to the expressed feelings (rather than the facts) by ' accepting ' comments at appropriate times. For example, when there is a pause in the outpouring, he might remark, ' It all seems so empty now, especially as you remember the lovely times you used to have together ', assuming of course that this was the kind of feeling that was being expressed. Care should be taken not to add anything to the feelings or to distort them in the response.

This is still not the best time for attempts at

reassurance, except the simple assurance of the Counsellor's readiness to ' be with ' the bereaved person and to share in the difficult adjustment. This is better offered in action than in words, and it may involve assistance beyond ' first aid in counselling '. This is also not the best time for specifically religious reassurances beyond those given in the funeral service. Such reassurances can well be offered personally after the emotional release has had a reasonable expression. If such religious assurance is asked for at this time it may be appropriate for the Counsellor to respond quite simply with a remark such as ' You and I both know that God is Love, and that whatever we may have to go through in life or in death we are surrounded and sustained by that Love. If we believe that, do you think we could leave the perplexing details where they belong, in the " Better Hand " than ours ? '

During the first few weeks after a bereavement the grief-stricken person may be encouraged to talk about the loved one by simple remarks which leave the person free to do so or to avoid doing so. If the Counsellor has known the deceased he might offer such a remark as ' I've been thinking a lot about him and his friendliness, he was such a fine person '. If the Counsellor was previously un-acquainted with the deceased a more appropriate approach might be ' I wish I'd had the privilege of knowing him ; he must have been a good friend to many people '.

In the same way, letters of condolence will generally be most helpful when they express fellowship and encourage loving remembrance. ' You have been very much in our thoughts at this time ', ' We have many happy memories of him ', and ' I wish I had been able to see more of him ' are examples of helpful expressions. If any reassurance seems appropriate it is best given in the simplest terms, avoiding such clichés as ' Time heals all wounds '. A simple quotation may be appropriate, such as :

' You were born together and together you shall be for evermore

You shall be together when the white wings of
   death scatter your days,
Aye, you shall be together even in the silent
   memory of God.'
(From *The Prophet*, by Kahlil Gibran, Heinemann)

3. *Somatic Symptoms.* As with any intense
feeling, grief will produce a number of bodily
symptoms. There will generally be loss of appetite
and there may be a heavy feeling or even pain in
the abdomen, dryness of the mouth, lassitude, and
muscular weakness. Headache, insomnia, extreme
restlessness and inability to sit still are common.
If necessary these will receive medical attention,
but the Counsellor might well have the opportunity to reassure the grief-stricken person that
these symptoms are normal and generally temporary.

4. *Specific Emotional Reactions.* At some time
in the process of working through the grief reaction
the person may experience one or more quite
specific emotional reactions.

(a) *Depression* is inevitable, and may last for
some time, especially when other difficulties and
hardships are added to the grief. It is important
that the Counsellor should avoid attempts to
' cheer him up ', or to rush him into a lot of
activities ' to take his mind off his trouble '.
Frequent brief visits, small, helpful services, and
a readiness to listen, are generally the most
appropriate ways of helping the person in this
distressing period of depression.

(b) *Loneliness* is another inevitable consequence
of bereavement. It is an inner loneliness which no
human company can fully overcome. The
understanding friend who is ready to be a good
listener rather than a good talker will generally be
of most help during the acute stage of this inner
loneliness until the person is ready to take up life
again and become involved in activities with other
people.

(c) *Confusion*, the inability to make decisions,
coupled with a general feeling of helplessness, is
best helped by standing by, assisting in various
ways, reassurance that this is generally temporary,

and possibly reminding the person that many decisions can wait until he is better able to give his mind to them.

(d) *A Sense of Guilt* is another common emotional reaction after bereavement. However much devoted service the person has given to the loved one there may be distressing feelings that it should have been better, or that there should have been more expressions of love. The Counsellor's most helpful rôle at this point is to listen and to encourage the full expression of these feelings. It is generally futile and may even be harmful at this stage to try to apply ' reason ', because the feelings are not open to reason or reassurance at this stage. Nor is it helpful to try to block the expression of feeling ' to reduce suffering '. Such attempts do more to help the Counsellor's anxieties than the sufferings of the bereaved person. A simple questioning comment, such as ' You feel that you really could have done more ? ' or ' You wish you had realized what was happening ? ', may help the person to ventilate his regrets, even those which may seem unwarranted. He will work through his distressing feelings better in this way than with any attempts at reasoning or reassurance, however tempting it may be for the Counsellor to make them.

(e) *Hostility* may emerge in many grief-stricken people, often with great intensity. It may be felt at the beginning, especially when there has been an obvious reason for it, such as in cases of culpable carelessness (the child killed by a drunken motorist, for example). It often appears some days later, when the shock and the emotional catharsis have been worked through to some extent. Here again the hostility may appear to be largely or wholly unwarranted. It is often directed at doctors, nurses, hospitals, attendants, relatives or friends who may have given the most devoted and competent service. The Counsellor's most helpful rôle at this point is again to be a good listener, and to give full encouragement to the expression of the hostile feelings, however inappropriate they may seem, without generally attempting to correct apparent misunderstandings. Such feelings are not likely to be modified by attempts at rational argument or defensiveness. With the Counsellor's acceptance and his encouragement of the unburdening the person will come to clearer insight in due course. Even if the hostility is well justified the person will be able to work through it most constructively in this way. The Counsellor needs to be careful, however, not to give undue encouragement to the hostility itself, as distinct from the expression of it. To accept the person's feelings need not imply that the Counsellor believes them to be justified. That is a matter for the person himself to work out, and the Counsellor is out of his rôle when he sets out to be a judge. Over-encouragement of the hostility itself may result in its persistence in an unhealthy manner for an unduly long period and in morbid form. This is where Empathy ('I know how you feel') differs from Sympathy ('I feel as you do'), and Empathy is the most healthy therapeutic attitude.

5. *Idealization of the Beloved, or of the Situation before the Loss.* At the beginning of the grief reaction there may be an intense preoccupation with the loss, and a constant comparison of the previous situation with the present one. As the grief is being worked through there will often be an apparently irrational tendency to idealize the loved one and the previous situation, which may astonish those who knew him in life. For example, a bereaved wife who had previously been in continual distressing conflict with a mentally or physically cruel husband may come after his death to represent him as the paragon of all the virtues. This may be related to some of her guilt feelings, and it often represents a part of her unconscious defence mechanisms, together with the response to the cultural attitude of saying nothing but good of the dead. The Counsellor, recognizing this, will help best by listening and accepting, showing acceptance by some such comment as, 'You have many cherished memories of him and of all that you enjoyed together'.

These then are the common elements of the grief reaction, and some ways in which the Counsellor may be of positive help have been indicated. As time goes on, the grieving person may need some encouragement in his difficulty in taking up his usual patterns of living once again and facing up to the realities of his situation. This encouragement can be given more effectively when the Counsellor has been able to carry through with the therapeutic rôle as described. The minister may now have many opportunities of talking over with the person some of the meanings of death and the faith in immortality, ' the resurrection of the body ' as the Creed expresses it. This takes the discussion beyond the present limits of ' first aid in counselling ', and every minister and layman will have his own ways of approaching it. It may be said, however, that the more the person can be encouraged to express his own ideas and feelings the better. Listening and mutual exchange of ideas will generally be more helpful than a private ' lecture ' for most people. Referral for expert help may be considered when the depression or any other negative feelings appear to be continuing for more than a few weeks or when they appear to be increasing beyond any apparent justification.

Finally, a special word about the bereaved child may be appropriate. Children tend to go through the same kind of grief reaction as already described and because of their relative dependency they will generally need more demonstrative affection and support. An effective helping resource for children even more than for adults is the opportunity to express their feelings both verbally and by acting them out in their own particular manner, possibly with play materials. In a film released some years ago, *Forbidden Games*, a little girl, suddenly deprived of both parents in the German bombing of refugees in France, wandered aimlessly through the fields until she came upon some peasant children. They worked through the overwhelming disaster by playing with the gravestones in a near-by cemetery. Children respond very well to the emotional attitudes of adults, and they are best helped if the relevant adults can face the situation openly and honestly, expressing their grief and allowing the children to do so, and giving them the full opportunity to participate in the family's working through it. Above all, it may be emphasized that steady faith is likely to prove a most valuable and infectious quality, and children can respond to it with more insight and courage than generally expected, as long as they have the security of being loved and allowed to share in the family crisis. Many children feel isolated and alone when attempts are made to ' protect ' them from grief at the very time that they need the experience of family unity and solidarity. To assist people in grief is a valuable and far-reaching service, which can be offered by any minister or layman who prepares himself for it.

XI. Men Under Attack

BY THE REVEREND MICHAEL HARE DUKE,
CLINICAL THEOLOGY CENTRE, NOTTINGHAM

THE Christian, according to the New Testament, is expected to be different from other people by the fact that his love extends not only to his friends but to his enemies. The standard is set by Jesus himself.

You have heard that it was said, ' You shall love your neighbour and hate your enemy'. But I say to you, Love your enemies and pray for those who persecute you, so that you may be sons of your Father who is in heaven ; for he makes his sun rise on the evil and on the good, and sends rain on the just and on the unjust. For if you love those who love you, what reward have you? Do not even the tax collectors do the same ? And if you salute only your brethren, what more are you doing than others ? Do not even the Gentiles do the same ? You, therefore, must be perfect, as your heavenly Father is perfect. (Mt $5^{43 \cdot 48}$ RSV).

If we follow this distinction which Jesus makes between the natural man (' Even publicans and sinners do as much ') and the standard He sets for His disciples it seems that we have come to a very profound part of our Faith. Here in practical terms He is elaborating the overall command to aim at the divine perfection. Immediately we recognize that this is not something that we can do in our own strength. If we are to love our enemies, it will need not human goodwill but an invasion of divine charity into us.

Yet even this piece of theological perception has not effected the practical outcome. In spite of two thousand years of Christian teaching our response to a hostile threat tends still to be that of retaliation. At the level of international politics, this could be seen most tragically during the course of the last war. Only Bishop Bell of Chichester raised his voice in Parliament against the devastation of German cities by allied blockbuster bombing. Even now as we look back on the events of twenty years ago it seems that few consciences are stirred by our complete failure to heed the words of Christ. We have exacted from the enemies of those days reparation both economic and emotional. It has occurred to only very few that it is as appropriate for us to be contrite about the thousands who died under the weight of our bombardment of Dresden as it is to expect the Germans to be sorry for the hundreds who perished in Coventry. Put the matter to the average Englishman and for all his Christian background he will reply ' They started it ' or something to the same effect.

In the political field it certainly does not seem that we have any response except ' an eye for an eye '. When it comes down to our own personal experience few of us could claim to do any better. It is perhaps not so easy to define whom we mean by ' enemy '. We do not have many occasions to harbour actual hatred against an individual on the level of a personal vendetta. Yet this does not mean that we are without experience of hostility or do not need to ask what the Gospel means about turning the other cheek.

There are plenty of practical instances which we would recognize. An insult makes us bridle. We may not demand satisfaction in terms of the law, but few of us can avoid getting our own back in one subtle way or another. If we are the subjects of what we regard as a false accusation, we leave no stone unturned until our fair name is cleared. Sooner or later every Christian congregation has the unhappy experience of hurt pride needing to be assuaged.

Indeed a great many faithful men would feel that it was important that justice should be done and the slanderer brought to book. In pleading their own cause they would feel that they were on the side of the angels. This does not square with the assessment of such a situation in the first Epistle of St. Peter.

Servants, be submissive to your masters with all respect, not only to the kind and gentle but also to the overbearing. For one is approved if, mindful of God, he endures pain while suffering unjustly. For what credit is it, if when you do wrong and are beaten for it you take it patiently ? But if when you do right and suffer for it you take it patiently, you have God's approval. (I Pet 2^{18-20} RSV).

Here it seems that our notions of rudimentary justice are overturned. It is in the same vein that St. Paul writes : ' It is a very small thing that I should be judged by you or by any human court. I do not even judge myself ' (1 Co 4^3). The more one thinks about it the more radical a demand this seems to be on the part of Christianity that we should love our enemies. To understand its implications more clearly it would seem that we need first to look at the dynamics which underlie our responses to hostility and then to see what remedies the Gospel supplies for our apparently chronic antagonism.

It will perhaps be easiest to make our analysis not in general terms but by particular instances.

Let us imagine the case of a faithful member of a congregation who after some discussion of a Christian Stewardship of time has volunteered to visit an old person in his home. The contact begins well, the visitor is met with gratitude and feels a natural warmth at this appreciation. After a while, however, some circumstances outside his control prevent the visitor making his weekly call. In this he feels quite justified ; his business or his family have a prior claim on his time. In spite of his explanations, however, the old man he has undertaken to visit seems hurt and rejected. This is at first expressed by a chilly silence and then pours out in a whole torrent of complaint about the way people prove unreliable.

Here it would be all too easy for the original good intention to breed a harvest of dissatisfaction and hostility. The old man could be left with the sense of grievance that what was offered was not supplied. The visitor might well be heard saying that he had been ' put off that sort of thing for good '.

What exactly has happened ? The old man has

interpreted the absence of his visitor as a lack of caring: ' He did not think I was important enough to be bothered with '. What will give added force to this accusation is if his past experience has also been one of rejection. In that case the old man will bring into play all the bitterness that belongs to those earlier occasions as well as the present.

A trained case-worker or therapist would know how to receive this response. It would be a matter of understanding all that lay behind it. In ordinary life we do not pause to analyse what is happening with such care. The visitor is apt to take the attack at face value. Even so, it is possible that he will shrug his shoulders feeling vaguely, ' Old people are like that ', and continue his contact. In fact the content of his response will also be affected by experiences out of his own past.

It might be that his original offer of visiting had in it more than he realized. He could have been working out some of his feelings of guilt about his own parents and for this reason needed, more than he realized, to receive the old man's approval and gratitude. Or again he might himself be feeling unwanted and hoping by an offer of service to find that he belonged again. The possibilities are too many to list but in so far as the old man's hostility hits his helper on a sore spot, the chances of an understanding acceptance of the hostility are reduced.

From such a situation we can see that when a man has a good basis of security in a relationship, he can afford to be generous, understanding, and forgiving. Where he is feeling already on the defensive, he is liable to counter-attack.

The instances could be multiplied. The bitter complaints about ingratitude seldom come from happy contented people. They are voiced by harried, anxious souls who feed hungrily on other people's approbation of their good deeds. The man who goes to court in order to preserve, by an action for libel, his own reputation has not much faith in its intrinsic value. An insult can more easily be overlooked if you are certain that it is undeserved.

Our hostility is always the measure of our insecurity. Yet when we have said this we have not sufficiently described the situation for the insecurity needs to be understood as arising out of inner conflict. It is as though the person who is whole can cope with an 'enemy' who only impinges from without. The person who is divided finds that any attack is aided by a fifth column within and this is what makes it so dangerous. I only really notice an accusation of laziness from my parishioners if I already carry a load of guilt which drives me ceaselessly to work. Where this is the case I am almost bound to hit back at my accuser. By the same token I am likely to accuse others of laziness and be angry if they seem to get away with it.

The same pattern of finding one's own weakness in another can be seen in the case of a Mr. A. who came for help. He was suffering from an acute depression. The onset of this he related to an incident in a public lavatory where a man had made a homosexual approach to him. This he had fiercely repulsed with threats of sending for the police. In the course of exploring the reasons for his depression he discovered in himself a repressed homosexual interest. Part of him revolted from the idea of contact with another man ; another part, deeply hidden, felt it to be the only safe relationship. If we agree that his unconscious mind had recognized this all along, we can see the need for the outraged rejection of the approach from another. The man became his enemy because he was threatening to make an alliance with the inner truth.

I have taken this example because it is unlike the usual situation in personal 'enmity'. In most cases there is an objective hurt to be forgiven, a blow in the face, a slanderous statement or whatever it may be. Sometimes we feel that we can accept the hurt ; we do not excuse but we forgive. Where a person feels that the wrong is 'unforgivable' so that the enemy cannot be loved, inner and outer world seem to have combined. The genuine outer 'wrong' is linked to past, unhealed resentments. One must look for the hidden factors which contribute to making the event seem so full of peril and distinguish them from the actual hurt done. In the case we have quoted the ' wrong ' of the homosexual approach is minimal. A person's reaction to this could be various ; there might be for instance either interest, abhorrence or compassion. Because Mr. A. needed to respond with anger, one was led to assume some sort of inner conflict which was triggered by the incident. It proved to be himself that he was hating, not the man who had accosted him.

It is our thesis that this self-hatred which we have tried to demonstrate in the particular case lies at the root of every inability to love our enemies. If we cannot forgive ourselves it seems that we cannot forgive anyone else either.

What help is this conclusion to us for practical living ? From a psychiatric point of view it might suggest that each of us would be pleasanter to live with if we had gone to the roots of our own conflicts. The remedy would then be to embark on the long journey into the past where the trouble began. We should have to recover the experience of splitting off the part of our self which we felt to evoke such overwhelming disapproval. To put the situation into a simplified picture form we might imagine a housewife with a driving compulsion to tidiness and order. For years she might have used her energy in accusing her disorderly husband of making her life a misery. To accept him would possibly mean a recognition that what she was battling with was her own right to be untidy if she wanted. That we might find had been forbidden to her by the training her mother gave her about putting everything in the right place. Above all one would expect to discover a rigid pattern of toilet training with a sense that ' dirty girls ' were ' bad girls '. The ramifications in the web would doubtless spread much further into the personality but for our purposes the simplified description will suffice to show how a present way of behaving links back to the past. It is perhaps possible to see how the woman we have imagined would have to deal with the idea of her own dominating mother who forbids her to be dirty, before she can tolerate her husband's untidiness.

Yet as soon as one begins to describe such a course of investigation, the impracticability of it becomes apparent. Who has the time or financial resources to embark on it? When a severe disability cripples a personality we are driven by necessity to go to its roots. This process is, however, to deal with one specific area. Its aim is to overcome the more obvious conflicts. In doing this much else may be uncovered and healed. Yet no one would claim for the most thorough-going analysis possible that it could overcome every insecurity. Yet as long as we have areas of insecurity left within our personality, they are the seed-beds of our compulsive hostility. Whoever touches on them is going to become our enemy.

It is in the idea of ' Security ' that the link with the Christian gospel seems to lie. We find our-selves driven to hatred and retaliation by the person who exposes that part of ourselves that we do not want to know about. We have hidden it because we had learned the lesson that it was an undesirable, unacceptable part and so, in the psychiatrist's jargon, we had split it off and repressed it. The heart of Christianity concerns the accept-ance, forgiveness and ultimate reconciliation of the ' bad ' people. Jesus was known as the friend of publicans and sinners, the people that society did not want to be identified with. Its appeal has always been to people who could risk admitting that at least inwardly they were in need of this reconciliation. As long as they retained the cer-tainty of their own goodness, the true Gospel had no message for them—' I came not to call the righteous but sinners to repentance ', said Jesus.

Those who have been able to accept this reassur-ance about the whole of their personality are beginning to be set free from the need to hate their enemy. He cannot reveal in them anything which is outside the love of God. Therefore, it is safe to acknowledge whatever emerges. If this is really true, then our enemy loses all his power and becomes the friend who helps us grow deep in our trust of God's grace. As his attacks expose new areas of sensitivity we shall by nature respond with pain, yet it is also possible that in the same moment we can learn more of ourselves in our weakness. This is not any longer something to be shunned or denied. Perhaps we can see new meaning in our earlier quotation from the Epistle of Peter. The unjust punishment is not now a piece of mortification which Scripture unfairly demands we shall bear. It is a springboard for new knowledge about ourselves and a deeper reliance on God, when once we have stilled the resentment of our natural selves.

The ' enemy ' becomes to us a vehicle of God. As we recognize this, we become able to love him in a way which transcends our natural hostility. It is not a matter of condoning his aggression or pretending it has not happened. We may well see it as love's duty to protest at what he has done, but we forgo our ' right ' to hit back and we can afford to do it because our ultimate security is established in God.

This must undoubtedly begin as a matter of inter-personal relations. One must recognize, however, that once this has been achieved, such an experience is bound to have far-reaching effects in every other sphere. If we find that a God-given security can set our own personalities free from a need to defend anxiously against every attack, what might not the effect be if we carried this truth into the field of politics or even inter-church relations ?

XII. The Threatened Nervous Breakdown : Part 1

Threatened Breakdowns Requiring Referral, and the Pastoral Care of Impending Reactive Depressive Breakdowns

BY DR. FRANK LAKE, M.B., CH.B., D.P.M., D.T.M., DIRECTOR OF THE CLINICAL THEOLOGY CENTRE, NOTTINGHAM

IF any individual has been brought to the edge of a nervous breakdown (other than by some sudden and obvious personal cataclysm like an untimely bereavement) the deprivations and conflicts leading to it have deep roots in his personality. These roots have their inward emotional aspects, extending back into the foundation years, as well as their outward interpersonal or social aspects, that spread out into contemporary affairs like horizontal roots. These last may be so apparently far removed from the patient s life as to be dependent on international politics or economics. Nearer or further away, the effects of contemporary horizontal, social influences are modified by those which come from the vertical taproots, going deep into the family past, to the third and fourth generation.

The full professional comprehension of all that goes to make up the human experience of a ' threatened nervous breakdown ' would require the use of a dozen languages appropriate to the various ' -ologies ' within which, for instance, the symptom of anxiety is integrated systematically. The conceptual levels are many, from biochemistry, neurophysiology, dynamic psychology, sociology, to existential philosophy and theology. The last of these ' -ologies ' describes the pastor's own professional field. He is, above all things, a pastoral theologian. So it may well be that he is not only the man to give first aid. At his preliminary interview he must decide whether confusion or dismay as to the ultimate meanings of life are integral to this man's threatened breakdown. If they are he must make this a prelude to a further interview. If people in trouble come to a pastor, it must be because their own intuition has led them to believe that at least part of the problem is in his field of concern. That intuition is important, and so we must consider pastoral first aid, not as a preliminary to sending the man elsewhere, but to dealing with him pastorally in greater depth, later. If there are conditions of breakdown in which this is not the case, the pastor will be able to recognize them in order to make the proper referral.

So let us say at once that if a troubled person goes to his minister for help in distress and is met with twenty minutes' ' first aid ' and nothing more, this will almost certainly be of little or no significance to the *solution* of his basic problem. If it pretends to be a sufficient pastoral response to a man who has, or feels he has, no one else to turn to, the mere application of ' first aid ' constitutes a case of pastoral malpraxis. There are few easier ways of insulting a layman who has been wrestling for months over a life problem, than to have it solved by a cocky minister in a few minutes.

There are, of course, cases of ' threatened mental breakdown ' which are disorders of the mind, which in our culture are dealt with primarily by psychiatrists, as a branch of the science of medicine. I have slipped in ' mental ', instead of ' nervous ' here, to indicate the sort of distinction we need to make between ' psychotic ' and ' neurotic ' breakdowns. In psychotic and organic conditions something other than, or more than, unacceptable changes of emotional state separate the patient from his usual ability to enter into meaningful conversation with others. This is no place to go into detail, though these are details every clergyman should be familiar with, on the basis of which he will decide that in certain cases pastoral dialogue cannot usefully proceed until psychiatric treatment has restored the patient to his powers of attention and comprehension of the spoken word.

The Severer Cases of Depression

There are severe depressions, of the kind that are usually referred to as ' endogenous ', which require psychiatric help. Since the patient is usually retarded to the point of total rejection of conversation, or at best to stubborn-seeming monosyllables, it is plain that any ministry of the word is gravely limited in its effectiveness. There are other pastoral ministries, however, the non-verbal communication of concern in the countenance, and the willingness to wait in friendly silence, neither going away nor pressing talk upon the patient, which may be much more effective than we are allowed to know at the time. But we cannot depend on this and must regard this condition, which typically wakes a man from 3 a.m. to 5 a.m. in a gloom which may not lift till noon, and takes all pleasure out of the rest of the day, as a medical emergency in which psychiatric referral without delay is imperative. Effective symptomatic remedies exist, in E.C.T. and drugs like Tofranil, to shift this dark mood of total gloom from the forefront of consciousness. Then communications can begin again, the pastoral one among them.

The Schizophrenias

Similarly, in schizophrenia, the pastoral dialogue is curtailed by the illness. In so far as pastoral care depends on words spoken and understood in the usual way, on experiences referred to in a common fund of experience, as deliberations and intentions validly arrived at and able to be consistently remembered and carried out, pastoral acts in these sufferers are liable to be broken up and interrupted by the intrusion into daytime consciousness of the bizarre dream-like world of the unconscious and its bewildering archetypal symbols and events. Any man not equally disturbed can recognize these alien and irrational elements, sudden blocks and uncanny jumps in the conversation, quaint and strange associations of ideas, delusions, hallucinations and so on, so that he has no doubt that the doctor ought to be called in. Pastoral first aid consists in little more than a quiet holding conversation, attempting to follow the wild goose chase of the patient's talk with some kind of sense-making response, if you can discover it, and saying so kindly and politely if you can't. You can often make better sense by looking at the emotions on the face than by listening to the words as sentences. Before long the doctor will be on the doorstep.

Toxic Psychosis and Changes of Personality due to Organic Diseases

Finally, in states of toxic psychosis or organic deterioration leading, for instance, to delirium or dementia, the powers of the mind are temporarily or permanently in abeyance. The patient may be disorientated as to the time, the place, his own person, and yours. His mind and memory are decisively, often gravely, impaired. He may be in, or on the edge of, delirium, struggling to get into his clothes to go to work several years after he has retired. These, too, are obvious breakdowns which the G.P. is almost certainly attending to already, or soon will be. In all these cases it is likely to be the family that benefits from pastoral care, and that isn't to be thought of in terms of first aid, but of prolonged support given or arranged for. As for the patient, the pastor continues to give his support throughout the illness, up to the level of the patient's capacity to use his help. Even where verbal comprehension is lost we must not infer that non-verbal, symbolic, personal and sacramental acts cannot reach to the ' heart ' in helpful ways.

The Nature of Threatened Nervous Breakdown

Now that we have mentioned the main sources of breakdown that demand immediate psychiatric help, and the kind of pastoral first aid that knows how to hold a telephone in one hand and talk to a confused man in gestures with the other, we turn to the great bulk of threatened nervous breakdowns which are nothing more than crises in the course of personality difficulties and disorders, of neuroses (that is to say, fixated emotional difficulties), of character problems, personal conflicts and inadequacies, fears, scruples, compulsions, irrational fears, bad tempers, bad habits, addictions, ' evil thoughts ' of a cruel or envious kind, insoluble marital problems and intolerable stresses at work. These are in us all, more or less, but from time to time the unstable life situation of which they are the cause or the result, or both, becomes even more precarious in its balance and we become aware of this. We feel on edge, at the end of our tether. Can we define what it is that is going on here ? Can we express what these breakdowns really are, so that we can better judge what immediate pastoral help is indicated ?

It is a fundamental point of all modern thinking on this subject to recognize that ' nervous breakdowns ' (like ' psychosomatic illness ') is an omnibus term (semantically meaningless—the nerves have not broken down) accommodating all kinds of professionals who want to work on it and give to it, or to the parts of it they are trained to deal with, names, so as to integrate their knowledge systematically. Had the academic theologians not moved out of the serious study of pastoral theology in relation to sick people, theology would now have as significant a stake in ' nervous breakdowns ' as psychology or pharmacology. Maybe the integration of the integrated subsystems waits for theology, not for the first time in the history of man's knowledge of himself.

A nervous breakdown is threatened whenever ' bad ' aspects of the personality, the negativities which threaten some aspect of his self-affirmation, whatever he regards as dangerous, weak or wicked, over-anxious or over-angry, too meek or too murderous, begin to emerge from hiding to upset the uneasy *status quo*. Some of these could be described as *deprivations*, feelings of emptiness or meaninglessness, worthlessness, nothingness, hollowness and the like, connected directly with anxiety, panic, dread, or fear. Others would theologically be described as *depravities*, destructive rage, hatred, envy, jealousy, greed, and lust. The interaction of complex intra-psychic forces and of external factors leads to a breakdown of the existing defensive pattern. In therapy we are continually talking about ' re-establishing the defences ' which is a psychiatric way of implying that in everyone there are buried experiences of mental pain and violent reactions to them which are always undergoing an active process of burial, by repression and other defensive methods. Breakdown threatens when this process fails, in a number of ways :

(i) By the emergence of some of these negativities from the unconscious for the first time, threatening the brittle cosmos of the conscious mind with chaos.

(ii) By the risk that this hitherto private view of our ' badness ' may leak out so that other people get to know about it, upsetting our external relationships with the risk of destroying them. The fear that secret ' sin ' will become known, combined with a fear of confession, is a potent source of threatened nervous breakdown.

(iii) By a change in the external situation which hitherto permitted, indeed perhaps encouraged, the expression of certain ' bad ' qualities as if they were good. That is, when a neurotic collusion or manipulated situation comes to an end (as when a wife with unconscious guilt has needed a bad, drunken husband to assuage her guilt by punishing her cruelly. If this arrangement ends in separation, the new situation will force her to face her unmitigated guilt, and him to face his insufferable cruelty ; that is why such couples usually stay together like limpets.)

(iv) By a change in the internal situation whereby the customary pie-crust of repression becomes thinner or cracks up. This pie-crust, roughly identifiable as the super-ego, normally splits off the bad negative aspects from consciousness. Further to that, it insists on reprisals and reparation. The personality is forced into over-compensation against all the ' bad ' negativities, depravities, and deprivations, leading to a compulsive pattern of everyday behaviour which is in total reaction to all that is going on inside, producing exactly the opposite effect. This gives force and intensity to the denial, equal to the intensity of the inner badness which must be concealed. (Prudery becomes the reaction pattern formation covering up inner lust, just as meek submissiveness is the required reaction to inner rage.) Any serious upset of this internal dynamic system of controls, concealments, and restitutions is experienced as threatening and may lead to breakdown.

(v) By a combination of events, external and internal, in which the negative aspects are re-awakened and intensified, while the repressive, restraining aspects are weakened by exhaustion or illness. A most unsatisfactory life situation both exacerbates the internal negativities and diminishes the energy available to repress them. If we give time to listen, we shall learn about something in the last few weeks or months, at home, at work, or even at recreation, that has reactivated one of these bad emotions, not just on one level, but on two. On the first level, a quite natural present-day emotional reaction occurs. But this has resonated or reverberated down on to a second level, into buried samples of the same kind in the ' bad ' experiences of babyhood. These jostle into consciousness, along with all the now inappropriate infantile reactions and defensive fantasies to which they originally gave rise. This accounts for such things as excessive eating, drinking, and smoking, which are entirely inappropriate responses to adult anxiety, but quite understandable in terms of the excessive oral needs of the internalized infant in its reactivated insecurity. This second level of emotional reaction from buried infancy is more fundamentally disturbing to every system of body-mind interaction. You feel really upset.

The actual onset of breakdown occurs roughly at the moment when these all-or-nothing, built-in responses to long-buried painful experiences are resurrected into consciousness so violently that they break down the retaining wall within the mind, and burst like a torrent of angry waters into consciousness. These can be described in the language of the Psalmist or in the language of the clinician. The symptoms are those of mounting tension, apprehension, edginess, touchiness, irritability, fear of disintegration or of some unmentionable mental ' crack-up ' ; and as the thing builds up, there is an uncanny dread, with fears of unreality and loss of the self, or some of its essential qualities. In parallel with these mental disturbances are the physical symptoms of trembling or shaking, palpitation, cold sweating, tension headaches, tight bands round the head or chest, nervous dyspepsia or indigestion, nausea at the thought of food, ' butterflies ' in the stomach, urgent ' calls of nature ', restlessness and the like. If these ' physical ' symptoms due to autonomic disturbances are at all severe, the doctor can always give useful first aid by way of a tranquillizer or sedative to take the edge off these most distressing feelings. And a skilled pastoral approach which deals with some of the important contemporary sources of anxiety, and may explain simply how the symptoms are due to the reawakening of long-buried anxieties, will have the same pacifying effect.

As the moment of crisis approaches threateningly, there is a characteristic exacerbation of defensive counter-measures. Whatever defences against inner badness the personality is accustomed to use, are now considerably overdone. More strenuous efforts to suppress or repress or lean over backwards against the inner negativities are demanded by the critical situation. The bad is more carefully hidden up and we work day and night to show to all men such a strenuous pattern of good behaviour, specifically denying the unacknowledged badness. By this means we hope to convince ourselves and others that we are not heading for a breakdown.

The man about to suffer a reactive depressive breakdown has, on the inner side, a mounting rage, lust, anxiety, distrust, and apathy. There is an actual though hidden weakness of the will to be good, with fears of worthlessness and feelings of despair. Just before the breakdown he is working overtime to produce exactly the opposite of all these, so assiduously that he can hardly take time off to go to sleep. Besides, it is in sleep that the hidden negativities tend to break through into an unguarded consciousness so that it is safer to stay awake. He has not yet reached the full collapse of depressive breakdown, though he is tired out with the incessant struggle of the pre-depressive conflict.

First Aid in Threatened Depressive Breakdown

Now when this man is himself a pastor, what treatment or advice constitutes good pastoral first aid ? Shutting his bad self indoors, the depressed pastor is now, in full view of his parish, pacing back and forth with an earnest look upon his face, on the balcony of his life. Perhaps he is as yet unaware of the energy he is using up every day in resisting the impulse to leap over it to his death. For many months he will tell no one, until perhaps he visits his doctor with a few physical symptoms. He may, late in the day, be forced to buttonhole one of his dog-collared friends, pouring out the tale of his burden of work, half-boastfully, half-complainingly. He is on the edge of a breakdown, but he cannot admit it. What he asks for and wants is solid appreciation, not advice to slow up. Why not ? He cannot slow up the pace of his good works, because they, and they alone, are shoring up the retaining wall, and if that cracked and gave way, all the deluge of his negativities would sweep over him, destroying the ideal image of a good religious exemplar, maybe for ever. So, the first aid he wants, possibly the only first aid he will accept, is such as will help him to maintain his religious front, and for this he will be grateful.

But must we not admit that if all that follows first aid by way of pastoral care is in this same dimension, it is a pyrrhic victory, gained at the expense of a potentially deeper Christian grounding in painful truth and brokenness ? One way of looking at this man's sickness is to say that he is ill because he is insisting on justifying himself by works in a world in which human beings are so constituted that such a life, seriously maintained until the end, cannot fail to lead to depression and death of the spirit. For the whole dynamic system is egocentric. The law has ceased to be creative. Used in this way it does not relieve his burden but crushes him to death. Cure, as he conceives it, is what makes him ill. Depressive dynamics can be looked to as an instance of ' iatrogenic illness ', that is, an illness caused by misguided and inappropriate efforts at healing. Two worlds are in conflict within the sufferer. The world of law opposes the world of grace. The old way is in irreconcilable conflict with the new way of being rightly related to God and to one's self, and thence to all the work that has to be done. Both worlds use a common language, with apparently equivalent words. But the same words take on a totally new dynamic reference and meaning as we jump from the one world to the other.

Here again we see that all the primary words that parsons use are polarized by the dynamics of this and every situation of impending breakdown. The pre-depressive man, under the law, conceives of ' peace ' as the world gives it, only as a reward for work well done. But ' peace ' with God and with one's self in the Christian context bears a negative relation to this work-centred drive. God's peace is a gift, denied to those who think they can earn it. ' Don't use much theology in counselling,' a bishop was recently reported as saying at an evangelical conference. He tells me he was misreported. For it is impossible to speak of God's peace in counselling a man on the edge of depressive breakdown, or to lead him to that peace, without somehow alluding to the theology epitomized in that devastating text of Paul in Galatians 5[4]. Without question, this brother is trying to get rightly related to God, that is, to his true source of being, by doing what the law, even though it be God's law, commands. To do this, according to Paul, is simply to ' cut yourself off from Christ and put yourself beyond the reach of His grace '. Moses can be faithful in all his duties in the household of God but at the end of every day he remains a servant. He is never a son. But we are sons, by the gift of Christ, and this constitutes our being, apart from our works, so long as we maintain to the end the faith and trust with which we began (Heb 3^{1-6}). As Charles Simeon used to counsel the depressed, ' You stand in need not of effort, but of affiance '. Rest, trust, and abiding are the requisite verbs. The pastoral theological therapy for the over-driven depressive man works on the very same dynamic principles as the psychiatric therapy, which consists in rest and all that makes for rest, and then a gradual re-creation in all systems. To rest, in despair of oneself, in the loving Being of God, on the invitation of Christ, is possible, for the Holy Spirit makes it so. I think back on many occasions when, within the course of two, or two and a half, hours, a priest or minister, threatened with depressive breakdown, has told me his whole tale and has moved, in the last half hour or so, through into this gracious peace. If we define first aid as that which must be done in under half an hour, I would find myself totally at a loss. But if I am allowed two and a half hours, and perhaps an hour on two or three subsequent occasions, though this may not be necessary, then first aid, so conceived, can conclude the whole operation of clinical pastoral care in threatened reactive depressive breakdown.

Judging by the treatment I receive when I am rôle-playing the part of a Christian on the edge of depressive breakdown, many priests still tend to take up judgmental attitudes and tell me what I ' ought to have done ' or ' must try to do '. ' I must try not to be depressed. I must try to help someone. I must be more particular about my prayers. I must redouble my efforts not to think angry thoughts or impure thoughts. I must go steadily on without self-pity. I must be more diligent, dispelling tiredness by a little extra hard work. I must make a rule and keep it more diligently.' This may be excellent religious first aid. It is so contrary to psychiatric practice as to account for the desire of many psychiatrists to keep such priests out of their wards. And they should be kept out. Because if the Christian gospel is true this kind of advice is damnable. Ministers, too, tend to shrink back from soul surgery, unsure of the validity of the radical gospel answer to religious depression. They proffer the kind of first aid their fellow hireling seems to be clamouring for. They tut-tut away the self-depreciation, giving as much praise as professional competitiveness will allow. They talk of his taking a week off, and ' then you will have more energy to tackle the job '. The priority is always the work, not the attitude towards God without which no Christian work begins to be possible. They reminisce about his past achievements and enjoy vicariously a meditation on his ministerial successes. If this brings him some little peace and joy, let us make no mistake, this is palliation, when a deeper perception of the dynamic impasse cries out for radical surgery within the soul. This is not to say that there are not many occasions when splinting, palliation, and temporary support of the old defences are not a wise tactical move. But the overall strategy, which may include a stepping back to jump better, knows its way through to the establishment of the kingdom of Christ *within* the areas of despair, apathy, anxiety, rage, and passion. The common run of ' pastoral advice ' deserves Job's derisive comment to his moralistic counsellors, ' Miserable plasterers are ye all '.

William Temple's dictum was never truer than it is here, that to discover the right answer to what look like short-term or trivial problems we have to go deep into first principles. No pastoral care of pre-depressive and depressed people, of however short duration, dare forget these complex but necessary first principles, and let them, as may prove practicable, guide our conduct.

XIII. The Threatened Nervous Breakdown : Part 2

Breakdowns in which Anxiety threatens rather than Depression

By Dr. Frank Lake, M.B., Ch.B., D.P.M., D.T.M., Director of the Clinical Theology Centre, Nottingham

There are people whose threatened nervous breakdown has no relation to depressive dynamics at all. They are not burdened by the law, duties, or a ponderous conscience. The ' badness ' which threatens them is not expressed as moral badness, but as the ' badness ' of loneliness or separation anxiety, of emptiness and meaninglessness. They respond with heightened sensitivity to external life situations which deprive them of good company, of durable friendships and exciting times, or warm and comforting emotions. These needs determine what they look for from the churches they attend. Though appearing to be ' terribly keen on ' a multiplicity of social meetings, they are, if the inner truth were declared, in flight from intolerably painful experience of loneliness, right up to the panic of infantile dereliction and dread. Or they are in flight from fixated experiences of weakness, emptiness, or exhaustion, of fearful and persecutory intensity.

In these rather extraverted people, the ' threatened nervous breakdown ' is an expression of the weakening of the retaining wall of repression which holds back the deluge of the primal terrors of the abyss, or the aridity of the wilderness. Their natural response to this weakening of the dam is to intensify the activities which have always been in reaction against the specific forms of ' badness ' or ' negativity ' to which they are prone. They attend more meetings than ever, injecting more apparent enthusiasm into them. They ' can't stand ' those who cannot work up an equivalent or superior ' keenness '. This ' keenness ' tends to express itself also in the sharp cutting edge of their criticism of others. The fact is that their peace and joy have been, almost from the beginning of life, negated by fearful inner loss of being or well-being, as persons in relation to others. They cannot tolerate the emergence of these wounds to the self, for they damage the identity, seemingly beyond repair. So their life now must be driven to deny what life was then. The original negation of peace must be itself negated so as to restore something that can be called peace, but is really nothing of the kind. How can you be at peace when the feeling can be maintained only by the denial of intense inner anxieties ? So, for all their seeking and all their striving for peace and joy, the end result is not God's peace, but strenuous human denials of peace denied. Their joy is excitement and enthusiasm, restless and impatient, not the deep joy of the beloved, daily renewed in faith and patience.

What, then, is true pastoral care for people like this, in whom, in spite of their exacerbated zeal to potentiate and elevate religious sensation, a breakdown of the whole process has become imminent ? To palliate would be, perhaps, to arrange for a revival mission, or move to a keener church with more of what it takes to keep loneliness and emptiness at bay. It would be quite mistaken to despise this kind of move. My experience is clear that at times repression is re-established by bigger and better enthusiasms, and the defences are re-established. But where deep anxieties are concerned, the doctor's tranquillizers are now in strong competition with anything the clergy can do by way of palliation and the re-establishment of the defences.

Is First aid in These Cases Necessarily Confined to Palliation and the Re-establishment of the Old Defensive Patterns of Life ?

If you only have an hour, I would say it all depends on your judgment as to the spiritual, mental, emotional, and physical health or ill-health of the person requiring help, which includes their readiness or capacity for insight, and the quality of the interpersonal relationships around them. If the symptoms of distress are at all severe, you may need to refer the parishioner as a patient to his doctor, in the hope that some medicinal help will reduce this distressful factor sufficiently to permit the patient to give his mind to the discussion of the personal problems which presumptively lie behind the symptoms. But it may well be that as a result of the pastor's patient and attentive listening to the sufferer's tale of trouble, these physical and emotional symptoms of distress decline considerably within the interview. This often happens when a good rapport is established. Listening of the right sort is the basis of first aid in clinical pastoral care.

If the first interview has this beneficial effect, it would be very poor pastoral practice to stop there. This person is evidently in the category of those whose anxiety is allayed by friendly and confidential conversation, often with a confessional element in it. At this point we come upon an important discrimination.

In threatened breakdowns we discern an often sharp division between the patients who clamour for pills to rid them of the distress, and those who are deeply relieved, and usually brush a tear away when they discover that you settle down to listen to them without an eye on the clock. The first group come to clergy for healing magic. Their god is a *deus ex machina*, whose job is to deliver them from this or that painful symptom. There have been priests and ministers who could dance to this tune, the intense, ecstatic sort who can pressure a devoted follower into the denial of any symptom. They need each other. But this tends to psychological collusion of neurotic needs, the ' gruesome twosome ', not clinical pastoral care. Better leave such patients to the doctor's pills until the hope of that kind of cure has fallen sick and died of deferral. If sacramental acts such as the Laying on of Hands or Holy Unction are offered to such people their sole interest is ' Will it work ? ', meaning ' Shall I get rid of my symptom ? '. This does not invalidate such acts, but it can drag their essentially personal meaning into the gutter. Neither we nor they can stop God working in gutters, if good can come of it. But what is ' good ' and what is ' bad ' in such cases ?

The ' symptoms ' of ' illness ' in such patients are more accurately defined spiritually if we call them ' signs ' of ' health ', because they are indexive of a strong discontent at the impoverished life of this otherwise shallow and totally extra-verted personality. For so long as she (for pastors it is oftener ' she ' than ' he ') runs away from the symptoms they tell her lies, but when she does an about-turn and faces them as signs, however dreadful, of true needs which can be met only by true personal resources, at whatever abysmal depth they exist to be helped, then they are signs that tell the truth and lead to the truth.

So we see that the existential experience of threatened nervous breakdown is itself polarized by the Gospel. Its potentiality for great good or great evil depends on the point of view, on the vision, on what we see in it, and what we see through it, and our response to this perception. ' Lord this is a most humiliating weakness, I've asked you three times to get rid of these symptoms. If you let them persist in one of your chief apostles, might not other people doubt your power, or your love, or both ? ' ' Dear Paul,' replies the Divine Counsellor, calling him alongside to take His point of view, ' You had better keep it. It is a sign, not a symptom ; a signpost ; a need with implica-tions ; a reminder to keep your eyes, your mouth, your heart open towards me, for strength. You won't lose by it, you'll gain, immeasurably.' Paul's strength is now *in* weakness, not by riddance of the weakness. *He* is now a sign of the thera-peutic paradox, of the eschatological dimension of healing, of the fact that faith and hope find their fruition, both in ' the temporal now ', and in ' the eternal now ' which holds within it the ' then ' of the ultimate consummation of all healing. Which it shall be is a decision the Christian learns, sooner or later, to leave in the hands of his King, ruling from the Cross.

Those same regrettable weaknesses of Paul's are now at the other pole of his experience, not of shame-in-shame, but of glory-in-shame. 'Most gladly, therefore, will I glory in my infirmities, that the power of Christ may rest upon me' (2 Co 12⁹, and see also 1 Co 2³, 2 Co 1⁸⁻⁹). So, he remains weak, and his thorn in the flesh does not abate ; distresses of all kinds, external and internal, press upon him. But irremediable suffering takes on an entirely new dynamic meaning. It works together with the other more obviously good things, for good.

When we set out to give first aid to someone on the edge of a breakdown, we do not know on which of these levels we ought to be working. 'We do not even know what to pray for.' That is a Romans 8 experience, not mentioned in the earlier chapters of Christian experience. But the Spirit Himself makes intercession for us both, His groaning reproducing the groaning of the Saviour, alongside the groaning of the afflicted one before us, and maybe our groaning also. Better that by far than proud and foolish words of moralistic advice. This Holy Spirit, searching the hearts, knows the will of God in each particular instance. We shall be shown on which level it is possible to work. On the first level our hope is that Christ, in power and glory, will heal by eradication of the evil we suffer under. The second level claims and comes to the abiding certainty that Christ, crucified through weakness, yet lives in the power of God (2 Co 13⁴), that His glory is obscured in shame and scorn only to unseeing eyes, and that this Christ of the paradox has healed us *now* by impregnation of His crucified and risen life, and by transformation of the nett effect of the evil we still suffer with, but no longer under.

It is, I believe, these facts which are the real contribution of Christian pastoral resourcefulness in time of threatened breakdown. Those whose initial response is to demand magical or medicinal cures, or to project the trouble on to some organ of their body, or even on to their friends or acquaintances, rejecting insight and the need to take a long look at inter- and intra-personal factors, are not likely to benefit from these paradoxical measures. Speak of these too soon to them and they listen, politely bored, and then ask, ' But, doctor, what about my symptoms ? ' These little pigs can't tell a pearl from a pill, so don't feed them with pearls, or you only produce resistances which will be hard to overcome later. ' I know, but I've tried all that,' they say, when you speak of the immeasurable resources of God's transformation of evil, as it takes its place in us in obedience to its Master, Christ. They have been inoculated against truth.

But those who have some ' psychological space ', some spiritual depth, perception, insight, realism, introspective honesty, reflectiveness, and capacity for dialogue (these terms all overlap), may move very fast indeed to the point of the paradox. The Spirit of Truth has long been working with them and they recognize you as a servant of this truth. Thus encouraged, they turn their back on the battlefield of competitive attention-seeking, of clinging, of thirst for sensational immediacy, of security operations, testing love by the willingness of friends to respond to an incessant touch-hunger or hunger for sight, of panic slammings of the door behind them that leads down to the unknown dread. Instead, in Christ, they turn away from the external world, which, so far as they are concerned, Christ has already left, to go ahead of them into its loss, and opening the door, they walk down the road they have always avoided.

Here we move into the pre-verbal world where metaphors are appropriate. Putting a hand into the impalpable hand of Christ, keeping their eyes, in the total darkness, upon the brilliant invisible light constituted by the certainty that Christ, too, is in this dreadful place, they move forward. So they walk into the valley of the shadow of death, or experience themselves as lowered under the waters of a second baptism of mental pain, threatening still, but not so threatening that they cease to trust the hands in which, by faith alone, they lie. The fires of torment, the dry, thirsty exhaustion of the wilderness, the attack of the demonic, of witches, scorpions, monsters, snakes, the lot, however the mind represents symbolically **its** primal injuries to trust in the source-person, who never came until too late to snatch a baby from the hell of non-being, none of these can turn him back. Threats to being by non-being cannot prevail, because the Source of all Being, who fills all things, fills all hells and all places of torment.

The language of the Psalmists comes into its own. Church people have forgotten that the psalms (22, 44, 66, and 88, for instance) represent experiences that still happen to people. Waves and storms, pits and wilderness, fires and dragons, are the universal language of the unconscious, revealed in breakdowns. He is a happy man whose pastor knows how to use the psalms on this occasion, and relate the syndromes of affliction they refer to, to the living theology of the New Testament.

So we see that the threatened nervous breakdown is itself polarized by the Gospel. As soon as the Christian realizes that Christ's next appointment with him is not in the world of finitude, touch, or sight, but in the depths from which flight is no longer necessary, precisely that which threatened him throughout his life becomes that which invites him as a pilgrim to proceed on his journey, in Christ, to meet Christ, in the total ' darkness ' of the ' absence ' of God, for this is an authentic mode of the vision of God which is the end of our human journey.

Threatened Breakdown due to Commitment Anxiety

We have little space to comment on the threatened nervous breakdowns which derive, not from separation anxiety or fear of emptiness, but from commitment-anxiety, and fear of dependence on others for sustenance in intimate matters. The same principles apply. Breakdown threatens them when they attempt to leave the ivory towers of detachment, whatever their content (whether intellectual, mystical, philosophical, gnostic, or some other niche for emotionally reserved persons), with intention to commit themselves to union with some individual or fellowship or binding promise in the world of people with bodies. They tend not to seek counsel and dislike being known intimately. The counsellor, if there is one, must move with a very light, no-touch, no-shoving approach. Secular counselling may interpret the difficulty in terms of approach-avoidance conflicts. The counselling of schizoid personality breakdowns cannot be summarized in a few sentences. (In my recent book the chapter on this subject alone runs to three hundred and seventy pages.)

Palliation aims to restore the defences, propping the good fellow up again behind his barricade of books. The Christian cure proposes a journey from compulsive detachment into union with God and with others in incarnate relations, in spite of the threat of breakdown as the man climbs down into the old abyss and up again on the other side. First he meets the area of commitment-panic, modified by the power of Christ's commitment-agony in Gethsemane. Then he is exposed to the dark night of the spirit, the area of dread and the demonic, in the same Christ's agonal power of endurance. Finally, he moves up through the belt of separation-anxiety, endured by the virtue of his Lord's dereliction on Golgotha.

This may be a long journey. We move no faster than we are helped to move. We are acted upon rather than acting. Even so, a Christian's nerve may fail when, at some sudden twist of the road, he comes upon an unexpectedly terrible view—of himself. Spiritual directors should know of these sudden turns and shocking sights, even though they have not yet travelled that way. They can authenticate the new direction and restore the shaken nerve. Spiritual directors and evangelical counsellors need to distinguish between the *break-up* of previously valid life patterns, as the abundantly healthy Christian enters a confused transitional stage prior to adopting a deeper way of relating to God and others, and the *breakdown* associated with ' spiritual ' emotional or ' physical ' illness. The turbulent and distressing *content* of the imagination is the same in both. Too often it is labelled, ' For psychiatrists only '. A mishandled ' breakup ' can become a ' breakdown '.

So, to conclude : threatened nervous breakdowns always consist in *painful truth*. Both pain and truth, in excess, or prematurely thrust upon a man, can be destructive. But to attend only to the one, and neglect the other, either way is bad pastoral or medical practice. Clergy feel ill at ease and become anxious dealing with the pain, as doctors do at dealing with the truth. That being so, we need not feel put out by the realization that our first concern is for the first-aid treatment of our own anxiety. Let us be prepared to admit that when an interview makes us very anxious, what we do by way of counselling may well be directed primarily to the treatment of our anxieties, not the client's. There is often a tug-of-war between the parson and the parishioner as to whose anxieties are to be treated. The laity are used to this situation in which they must permit the clergyman to treat his. That is why clergymen in this country are too little used in counselling, as yet.

Be prepared to stay with what is, with whatever the sufferer says, wherever it leads. Go with the sufferer to *his* place of torment. Don't struggle to drag him, even though he seems to want you to, on to your raft. Don't be tricked into giving advice, even if he asks for it, except perhaps in peripheral matters to set them aside so as to keep track on the main problem. Skill in non-directive responding can turn the conversation so that he makes the appreciations and the decisions himself. Follow the train of thought, don't pull him off on to yours, unless he is stuck in a groove. Don't be afraid of pregnant silences. Remember that thought is often slowed up. The wells of affliction are deep. It takes a long time to get the bucket up. Clerical wells are sometimes shallow, that's why the bucket comes up so quickly. Be prepared to share in the indecision, the doubt, the confusion and bewilderment, looking with the sufferer at what is. What ought to be can wait. God saves us *in* what is, not *by* what ought to be. Your understanding of the problem, and his, can wait. Perception comes first, conceptualization can follow. Know the soul thoroughly and, if first aid goes well, be prepared to give further interviews.

The principles of non-directive counselling make for good first aid. The practice of paraphrasing what the sufferer says, just to indicate that you have understood and are still with him, is well known and sound enough. It is so much better than the ' good advice ' technique that treats no one's anxieties but the parson's, or at times of those who wish to be confirmed in old unchanging patterns. You may not get round to the mention of specifically Christian resources within the ' first-aid ' period. Never mind. The concern to do this is a professional compulsion to do with clerical anxieties, not with the Holy Spirit. Job's comforters spent seven days and seven nights silent. Had they spent the next seven days and seven nights in the same silence, Job would have been spared a miserable experience of moralists talking beside the point.

Be prepared for anything. Immediate moves may be possible into those paradoxical experiences we have spoken of, which are the specifically Christian resource in threatened breakdown. So don't feel obliged just to re-echo the parishioner's sentiments, parrot-wise. Our model in clinical pastoral counselling is not the parakeet, but the *Paraklete*. Be in the power of the Holy Spirit, to come alongside and communicate the presence of God, as Romans 8 portrays Him and His work. This response, in us first, of willed brokenness, and ' active passivity ' in the clay-potter dimension, fits us, not so much for ' counselling ' as for ' paracleting ' those who are threatened by personality breakdown.

XIV. The Suicidal Emergency

BY THE REVEREND HOWARD J. CLINEBELL, JR.,
PH.D., PROFESSOR OF PASTORAL COUNSELLING,
SCHOOL OF THEOLOGY, CLAREMONT, CALIFORNIA

' More than a thousand people all over the world die
of suicide daily. . . . There is no country which is not
affected by the problem. There is no human being who
should not involve himself.'—Erwin Ringel, M.D.,
President, International Association for Suicide
Prevention.[1]

THERE is growing recognition among the helping
professions that the clergyman is on the front
lines in giving initial help to those in various
mental health crises, including the suicidal
emergency. This is true for several reasons : (1)
He is normally with people at the major pressure-
points in their lives at which serious problems are
apt to develop, *e.g.*, bereavement, sickness and marriage crises. (2) Many people spontaneously turn to
him when they find themselves going through
deep water, because they have felt trust in clergymen since early childhood. (3) The minister is in
continuing contact with many families. As a
family-oriented professional he deals directly with
the seedbed of mental and spiritual health or
illness. If he is tuned to the wavelengths of persons,
he often can recognize early-stage problems and be
an instrument of direct help or referral. (4) He
represents ultimate meanings, a community of
faith and concern, and the vertical as well as the
horizontal dimension of human existence. As
such he has a unique contribution to make to the
constructive handling of suicide and of those
aspects of every problem for which there is no
meaningful answer except in a spiritual frame of
reference.

In no mental health area is the minister's rôle
more crucial than in the prevention of suicide.
Each year some five thousand persons take their

[1] 'Suicide Prevention—A World-wide Obligation',
VITA, Newsletter for the Inter. Assn. for Suicide
Prevention, Jan. 1966, 2.

own lives in the British Isles. In the United States the figure is almost twenty thousand. For every person who dies by his own hand, eight attempt to destroy themselves and fail. Every attempt, successful or not, stems from person-damaging relationships and produces a wave of suffering in its wake. The minister who masters the skill of helping suicidal persons may save lives in both the biological and spiritual senses.

The clergyman's rôle has these facets : (1) Recognizing suicidal persons ; (2) Providing emergency help until an appropriate referral to a psychiatrist or suicide prevention centre can be made ; (3) Continuing pastoral care of the person ; (4) Pastoral care of the family ; (5) Helping the suicidal person fill the ' value vacuum ' (Viktor Frankl) at the root of his problem ; (6) Encouraging the development of community suicide prevention services.

Recognizing Suicidal Persons

Recent research has shown that suicide is seldom a sudden, unpremeditated act. Prior to attempting suicide the person sends out distress signals—his personal ' cry for help '. Suicide is often a desperate, distorted attempt to communicate with family members. The following behaviour or conditions are frequently associated with suicide :

1. *Obvious suicidal threats.* Verbal threats of self-destruction are the most significant warning signals preceding many suicide attempts. One study found that ' of any ten people who kill themselves, eight have given definite warning (often unrecognized except in retrospect) of their suicidal intentions '.[1] The old belief that ' people who talk about suicide don't commit suicide ' dies much more slowly than the countless persons who continually demonstrate its fallacious nature. The only safe axiom to follow is this, *all suicidal threats must be taken seriously !* Even if one has no intention of killing himself, but is only trying to manipulate others, he is profoundly disturbed and

[1] ' Some Facts about Suicide', Public Health Service Pub., Par. 85, 3.

needs psychiatric help. A person whose self-esteem is so depleted that he uses this deadly threat to cause others to care for him or do what he demands, is in dire need of both pastoral care and psychotherapy.

2. *Covert suicidal threats.* Persons who express feelings that life is empty and meaningless, who believe they are no longer needed, who wish they could ' go to sleep and not wake up ', are usually expressing suicidal or pre-suicidal feelings. Making plans for death can be a clue to impending suicide, particularly if accompanied by general unhappiness.

3. *Depression.* Psychiatrist Karl A. Menninger states :

' All deeply depressed people are potential suicides ! Many of the suicides ascribed in the newspapers to financial worry, disappointment, etc. are undoubtedly cases of melancholia; the victims would probably have recovered and gone on to spend useful lives had their condition been recognized and the proper steps taken. . . .' [1]

Depression may be characterized by general retardation in moving and speaking, or by tension and agitation. Other symptoms which may indicate depression include severe feelings of hopelessness, guilt and unworthiness ; chronic insomnia ; loss of appetite and sexual desire ; severe weight loss ; chronic apathy and fatigue ; social withdrawal ; loss of interest in previously-prized activities ; or a façade of exaggerated and brittle cheerfulness.

4. *Loss.* Persons sustaining crushing blows to their self-esteem or staggering losses (*e.g.*, by death, divorce, loss of job), may be suicidal during the ' reactive depression ' which ensues. In bereavement, the greater the frustrated dependency and hidden (repressed) anger toward the lost person, the more pronounced the depression. Pathological grief reactions—grief wounds that cannot heal because they are deeply infected by hidden guilt and rage—may lead to suicide, unless the poison is drained off the wound by skilled counselling.

[1] *The Human Mind* (N.Y.: Alfred A. Knopf, 1947), 122.

An absence of appropriate mourning, undiminishing grieving, continuing social withdrawal, drastic changes in behaviour, these are some of the symptoms of pathological grief. Psychiatric help is often needed in such cases.

5. *Chronic illness.* Those in severe pain and/or suffering from incurable illnesses may become suicidal. Severe feelings of helplessness, fear of being dependent (especially in men), and fear of intractable pain, may be involved.

6. *Mental disturbances.* Suicide has many causes. The underlying personality and relationship problems are varied and complex. Many different feelings are involved.

' In general, the suicidal person is in a disorganized, chaotic state. He feels helpless, hopeless and is looking desperately for assistance. He is usually anxious, confused, and frequently hostile. He feels lonely, alone, and rejected, and thinks that no one loves him. His suicidal behaviour can best be understood as an expression of his severe emotional distress.' [1]

All suicidal persons are emotionally disturbed, but the great majority are not mentally ill (*i.e.*, psychotic). However, some psychotic people do become suicidal. The same is true of alcoholics who ' hit bottom ' and find no help.

Providing Emergency Help

When the minister is contacted by or encounters a person threatening suicide, the goals of the helping process are these : (1) Establish a trustful relationship, (2) obtain the information necessary to evaluate the suicidal potential, (3) provide emergency emotional support, (4) prevent suicidal action, (5) help the person obtain medical treatment, a psychiatric evaluation and therapy, as quickly as possible, (6) mobilize the family's support and help.

If a stranger phones threatening suicide, the minister should communicate his concern and make every effort to build a bridge of trust which will allow the person to give his name and address, and

[1] *Suicide Prevention Centre, Manual for Handling Telephone Calls*, Los Angeles, Calif., 1963.

to accept the minister's offer to call immediately for a face-to-face talk. It is remarkable how much counselling can be done effectively by phone, in an emergency. Should the person be on the verge of gulping a handful of sleeping pills or pulling the trigger, it is crucial to keep him talking while someone who can intervene directly (family members or police) is alerted on another line. If the minister is contacted after a suicide attempt has been made, emergency medical help should be summoned immediately, or the person taken to the emergency service at the nearest hospital (to have his stomach pumped, for example). All attempters should receive psychiatric treatment, usually on an in-patient basis.

In counselling with the pre-suicidal person (as in all counselling), the first indispensable step is beginning to establish a trustful, caring relationship. This is done by listening with empathic concern to his story and responding to his feelings so that he knows the minister cares about what gives him pain. Whether a person is known or only suspected to be suicidal, it is essential to encourage him to talk frankly about this matter (after rapport is established). As one psychiatrist puts it, ' Talking openly about suicide often serves to rob it of its awesome and appealing quality '.[1] The fear that one may suggest suicide to a person who is not considering it is largely unfounded. Unless the person is encouraged to discuss whatever suicidal impulses he may have, they may be left reverberating in the hidden rooms of his psyche. One suicide prevention centre gives these instructions to its counsellors :

' Your own openness and willingness to confront the patient directly with the problem of suicide is very helpful in reducing the patient's anxiety. Inquire about the suicidal aspects of the behaviour matter-of-factly. Ask about prior attempts and when they occurred ; whether he is presently planning an attempt, and, if so, specifically what his plans are ; and whether he has the means available to carry out his plans.' [2]

---

[1] L. R. Wolberg, M.D., *The Technique of Psychotherapy* (N.Y.: Grune and Stratton, 1954).
[2] *Suicide Prevention Centre, Manual*, 4.

One reason for asking these and other questions is to obtain information that can help one sense the degree of danger involved.

It is well to know that the presence of any of the following factors increases the grim probability that the person will actually take his life : *male* (men attempt suicide less frequently but succeed more often than women) ; *older age group* (other things being equal, the older the person, the greater the lethality of a threat) ; *specific suicide plan* ; *the means* necessary to implement it ; *prior suicidal behaviour* ; *recent severe loss* ; *depression* ; *alcoholism* ; *lack of family or friends* ; *poor communication* with significant persons ; *defensive reactions by family* ; *mental illness*.[1] The deadliness of the threat tends to be greater as more of these factors are found to be present. In counselling with anyone who is threatening suicide, it is advisable not to let him out of one's sight until he is with some other responsible adult. In cases of obviously high suicide potential, this procedure is utterly crucial.

Although the death rate among older people who attempt suicide is considerably higher than among younger attempters, it is also true that suicide is much more common among adolescents than is generally known. A suicide threat or attempt by a child or teenager is invariably a cry for help and often an indication of severe (though often hidden) disturbance in his parents' marriage.

Counselling with a suicidal person should be done in an accepting, supportive and hopeful manner. By using his authority constructively, the minister can provide a positive, parent-figure for the person to lean on during his emotional crisis. If he has suffered a loss, he should be encouraged to talk about it in detail and to explore his feelings. Pouring out painful feelings often lightens the load of distress and lessens the chance of suicide. The reasons why the person is considering

[1] These factors are used in an instrument for evaluating lethality in suicide threats, devised by the Los Angeles Suicide Prevention Centre.

suicide should be discussed and the fallacies in them pointed out. The minister should offer his help by saying, in effect, ' I feel you can be helped and I want to work with you in finding a way of coping with your situation '.

The minister should use whatever approach is necessary to prevent suicidal action—persuasion, pleading, theological coercing, driving the person to a hospital, or, if nothing else is effective, phoning the police. An earnest appeal at least to postpone action, is often effective. *Minister* : 'Suicide may seem to you, in your present discouragement, to be the only way out ; but I am sure that we can find a better way. If you end your life, you will deprive yourself of the chance to find it. At least wait until we've tried.' If the person believes that his wife and children would be better off without him, he should be confronted in no uncertain terms with the clear evidence that suicide does untold psychological damage to most families, leaving them with a legacy of guilt and humiliation. The person should also be reminded of the satisfactions he will be forfeiting if he kills himself. Starting with his internal frame of reference, the minister should try to block suicidal action and, at the same time, arouse at least faint glimmers of hope. Special effort should be made not to increase the person's already crushing load of guilt.

The fact that a person tells a minister he is considering suicide is itself a somewhat hopeful sign. Anyone who communicates such intentions to a helping person possesses some desire for help, otherwise he would not bother to communicate. Research has shown that very few suicidal people are fully intent on dying. Most have conflicted motivation. They gamble with death, hoping at the same time that others will intervene and save them. The clergyman allies himself with the pro-life side of the life-versus-death struggle within the person.

During the first conversation with a suicidal person, one should attempt to obtain the names, addresses and phone numbers of relatives, close friends, and the person's physician. The person should be helped to understand that he needs all the help he can get from those who care about him, in weathering the severe emotional storm he is experiencing. After explaining to the person why it is necessary, it is usually wise for the minister to alert the appropriate adult family member to the seriousness of the problem and the imperative need for getting the person to psychiatric help immediately. The family should be encouraged to rally round the person with emotional support. This will not resolve the underlying family problems which usually are present, but it will undergird the person during his crisis. The family should be advised not to leave the person alone during the severe part of the crisis.

The belief that most suicidal persons remain so indefinitely and inevitably try suicide again is fallacious. Approximately sixty-five per cent. of those who make a first attempt unsuccessfully, do not make another.[1] Most depressions run their courses naturally. Suicidal crises caused by emotional upheavals, bereavement, and illness are usually temporary. If the person can be kept from suicide until the crisis passes, he will usually be grateful. (The period of greatest danger of repetition is the first ninety days after an attempt. The family should be advised of this fact.)

The physician is the clergyman's indispensable ally in all cases involving suicide threats as well as attempts. The doctor should be involved as soon as possible. Effective medical therapies are now available for lessening the awful pain of a depression. Whenever possible, an evaluation of the seriousness of a suicide threat should be made by a psychiatrist who can also decide what long-term treatment is needed. For the highly suicidal individual, intent on self-destruction, hospitalization is essential to protect him from himself. Suicidal threats and attempts in some cases are indicative of the onset of a psychotic illness requiring psychiatric hospitalization.

[1] Talk by R. E. Litman, M.D., Chief Psychiatrist, S.P.C., Los Angeles, 3.10.62.

Beyond Emergency Treatment

Most suicidal persons need three forms of help in addition to initial medical treatment—ongoing supportive relationships ; intensive counselling or psychotherapy to resolve underlying problems, strengthen self-esteem, reduce irrational guilt, and enhance relationships ; and an opportunity to find the only ultimate antidote for despair—faith.

On-going supportive relationships should include a rich measure of pastoral care, during and continuing after psychiatric treatment. In addition, each local church should train a ' pastoral care team ' of carefully selected, spiritually mature laymen, who can surround persons in crisis with a circle of loving concern. Persons who are engaged in lay ministries of this type, under the direction of their pastor, soon discover the deep satisfaction and personal growth that comes from being a vital part of a healing-redemptive community. The release of the tremendous untapped helping potentialities of maturing laymen is one of the exciting aspects of the contemporary ' lay renaissance ' in the churches.

The sixty-seven Samaritan Groups in the United Kingdom offer an invaluable referral resource which should complement the work of the local church with despairing, suicidal people. Many clergymen will find it helpful in their own crisis counselling ministries, and in their training of lay ' befrienders ' (the function which is at the heart of the Samaritan approach), to acquire a first-hand familiarity with the operation of the nearest Samaritan centre. If a minister's ability to do counselling is limited by lack of time or training, he would be well advised to refer persons he suspects or knows are suicidal to the Samaritans. The fact that skilled professionals are available at the Samaritan Centres as consultants and counsellors in difficult cases, adds strength to this lay-oriented programme.

The minister ought not to assume that because a person is out of his suicidal crisis, he does not need long-term counselling. The fact that the acute phase of the crisis is past may be precisely what will make it possible for the person to take a look at himself in depth, seeking to resolve the conflicts and problems which precipitated the suicidal episode. If the minister is not trained to do this depth-counselling himself, his rôle is to get the person to a competent counsellor or psychotherapist, and to encourage him to stay with the process long enough to derive the help he needs.

In working with suicidal persons, as in all pastoral care and counselling, the minister can maximize his effectiveness by utilizing community resources to the hilt. One of the bright spots in the suicide picture is the growing network of suicide centres in some fifteen countries. At present there are approximately one hundred and sixty of these. They are of two complementary types—those staffed by mental health professionals (e.g., the emergency ' walk-in ' psychiatric clinic) and those staffed mainly by laymen, trained and supported by professionals. The Life Line centres in Australia, as well as the Samaritan centres mentioned above, are outstanding examples of the latter. The clergyman has a responsibility to encourage the development of both types of community resources.

Helping the Family

Suicide is often evidence of a family illness. The whole family is usually in need of pastoral care. The hidden message in the suicidal threat or attempt has to be de-coded for the family so that they can deal with it. When the hidden message is essentially hostile, family counselling, perhaps family group therapy, is necessary to help them learn to relate in mutually-satisfying ways. If the minister has the time and training to do extended family counselling, he can render a valuable service to such troubled families. If not, he should assist them in finding skilled counselling in the community. Counselling with the family can be an important factor in preventing a suicide threat from becoming an actual attempt. Following an unsuccessful attempt, it is important that the whole family receive help in resolving the conflict that contributed to the suicidal behaviour. Improved family relationships can be a key factor in preventing a recurrence.

The family of the completed suicide almost always need extended counselling to deal with their swirling, painful feelings. Often their defensiveness keeps them from being open to the help they desperately need. The bereavement problems are almost always infected by powerful, hidden feelings of hostility, shame and guilt. The minister must employ all of his skill in facilitating the process of mourning so that the family may eventually work through the trauma and recover from the unfortunate stigma which our society still attaches to suicide. The basic strategy is to encourage the family to talk through their negative feelings rather than bury them and thus allow them to continue to fester.

The Unique Dimensions

The minister has a special stake in the problem of suicide because it involves questions of ultimate meaning. At the deepest level, the suicidal person's problem is a spiritual problem, an inner vacuum which renders him utterly vulnerable to despair. As has been suggested, the person needs a combination of therapies in order to recover. But recovery is not complete until the person has found a satisfying spiritual life, rooted in the conviction that existence has value and meaning. The lifting of the pall of depression which turns all life grey and squeezes the vitality out of everything, will restore the satisfaction of bodily functioning. But full recovery depends on finding what Erich Fromm calls ' a frame of reference and an object of devotion '. In the religious context this is the life of faith, experiencing the steadfast love of God and seeing our days as a gift entrusted to us to be used in His service.

As an expert in spiritual growth, the minister has a unique and indispensable contribution to make to the long-term helping of the suicidal person. His skills as counsellor and theologian must be blended in this aspect of ministry. With loving patience he must help the person discover and remove the inner barriers to full awareness of the reality of the spiritual purpose and power which is at the heart of the universe. Only thus can the troubled individual find a way of coping constructively with what Herman Melville described in that classic line from Moby Dick as ' a damp, drizzly November in my soul '.[1]

Counselling with suicidal persons is difficult, threatening and demanding. It confronts the counsellor with the ultimate issues of life and death, and with his own feelings about non-being. It reminds him of the damp, drizzly Novembers in his own soul. This is the place for the counsellor to begin—with an awareness of how *he* felt in his own periods of despair. Thus he may be able to enter the inner world of the suicidal person, walk with him through his dark valley, and perhaps help him find spiritual resources akin to those which the counsellor has discovered on his own inner journey.

Recommended Reading

N. L. Farberow and E. S. Shneidman, *The Cry for Help* (N.Y. : McGraw-Hill, 1961).
Pastoral Psychology, issues of Dec. 1953 and Jan. 1966 contain articles on pastoral care and suicide.
E. S. Shneidman and N. L. Farberow, *Clues to Suicide* (N.Y. : McGraw-Hill, 1957).
Chad Varah, *The Samaritans* (London : Constable and Co., Ltd., 1965).
(Readers may also like to know of Professor Clinebell's own book recently published by Abingdon : *Mental Health through Christian Community*. Editor's note.)

---

[1] I am indebted to Dr. E. S. Shneidman for indicating the aptness of this familiar line from Melville, as applied to the problem of suicide.

XV. The Clergyman's Rôle in the Alcoholic Emergency

By Howard J. Clinebell Jr., Ph.D.,
Professor of Pastoral Counselling, School
of Theology, Claremont, California, U.S.A.

In his counselling ministry, the clergyman serves those who spiritually lie crumpled beside our modern Jericho roads, beaten by the injustices and tragedies of life, and robbed of their hope and self-esteem. One important facet of this ministry is that of helping the alcoholic and his family. This is a vital opportunity to serve suffering persons in the spirit of one who was called ' great physician '. In the words which He quoted from Isaiah, to describe His ministry, it is an opportunity '. . . to proclaim the release for prisoners, recovery of sight for the blind ; to let the broken victims go free . . .' (Lk 4^{18}, N.E.B.). The alcoholic *and his family* become prisoners of his addiction, blinded and eventually broken by his spiralling compulsion. The minister who is equipped with *enlightened* concern and with counselling skills, can be an instrument by which the Holy Spirit heals their brokenness, bringing freedom and new life.

Understanding—The Indispensable Tool

Giving genuine help in the alcoholic emergency is a difficult, demanding assignment. To be of maximum effectiveness, a clergyman must have a clear understanding of the problem. The United Nations' World Health Organization defines alcoholism as ' a chronic behaviour disorder manifested by repeated drinking of alcoholic beverages in excess of dietary and social uses of the community and to an extent that interferes with the drinker's health or his social and economic functioning'. A person with alcoholism is anyone (whatever his age, sex, vocation, or social status), whose use of alcohol causes a continuing problem in any area of his living—his marriage, his job, his health, or his self-esteem. Even though his drinking damages things that are important to him, he continues to drink, showing that he has lost, to some degree, his *ability* to control his use of alcohol. This loss of control—the heart of the problem—results from an increasingly powerful psychological compulsion which eventually develops into a full-blown biochemical addiction. For reasons not fully understood by science, a certain percentage of drinkers lose their ability to handle alcohol.[1] Alcohol increasingly handles them—eventually distorting all areas of their lives.

In most cases, it takes from five to fifteen years of heavy drinking for full-blown alcoholism to develop. The loss of control is usually gradual—so gradual that the person himself is not aware of what is happening. Up to a certain point, the individual could probably stop drinking on his own. Past that point, outside help (Alcoholics Anonymous, medical help, pastoral counselling, etc.) is required. Once an addiction has developed, a person can never again drink in controlled fashion, even after prolonged therapy and abstinence. Some irreversible change has occurred in his organism. In this sense, alcoholism is incurable. It is, however, highly treatable. The goal of treatment must be to help the person live a satisfying, productive life *without alcohol*.

The clergyman should be able to recognize the three major forms of alcoholism, distinguishable by the drinking patterns of those so afflicted. The *steady drinking type*, the most prevalent, is characterized by increasingly heavy drinking, day-in, day-out, with frequent periods of intoxication lengthening into binges. The *periodic alcoholic* is usually abstinent between binges. His alcoholism probably is linked with manic-depressive mood swings deep in the unconscious mind. Periodic alcoholics are difficult to reach in counselling because they are so certain, between binges, that ' it will never

[1] Alcoholism is twenty times as prevalent as all other addictions combined in Western Europe, Britain and the U.S.

happen again '. The *plateau alcoholic*, the most difficult to identify, drinks more-or-less continually but, unlike the other types, seldom seeks maximum intoxication or goes on binges. Instead, he keeps his blood-alcohol level at a fairly constant level much of the time. His continual heavy drinking blunts the creative edge of his marriage and his job effectiveness, eventually producing problems which require counselling. Plateau alcoholism seems to be much more common among women than has been generally recognized. All forms of alcoholism are progressive in that they tend to grow steadily worse unless they are treated.

Alcoholism is an illness of the whole person—a physical, psychological, and spiritual illness. To say that it is an illness, as the W.H.O. and most medical authorities do, does not deny the existence of complex ethical issues in the problem. It merely refocuses them, putting the emphasis on the person's *responsibility for obtaining treatment*. This is the redemptive place to put it. The alcoholic is *a human being* with ' alcoholism '. His condition, like yours and mine, involves an incredibly complex mixture of sickness and sin, compulsion and accountability. But, if a minister moralizes with him by emphasizing his sin, the alcoholic is driven away from help and pushed deeper into the dark morass of his alienation from himself, others, and God.

Alcoholism is like a house with three stories. The bottom level consists of various personality problems producing high anxiety and low self-esteem. The pre-alcoholic values the anaesthetic properties of alcohol because it gives him temporary relief from his painful feelings. It is a self-prescribed personality medicine. The personality disturbance underlying alcoholism may be very severe (a psychosis, psychoneurosis, or sociopathic disorder), or relatively mild. One does not have to be a psychological cripple to become an alcoholic. The more one's social group regards heavy drinking as normal behaviour, the less personality disturbance is required to become addicted.

The second level is the addiction *per se*. By the time the alcoholic reaches the minister's attention, he is no longer drinking merely as a result of underlying problems (unless he is mentally ill). He is now drinking excessively to deaden the physical, psychological, and interpersonal agony resulting from previous excessive drinking. What originally was a symptom is now a ' runaway symptom ', a self-perpetuating vicious cycle which must be halted if the person is to survive. His drinking is now *compulsive*—i.e., driven by forces beyond his volitional control in his unconscious mind. It is *addictive* in that his biochemistry has become adapted to the presence of alcohol so that he experiences acute distress and craving when it is withdrawn.

The third level of the alcoholic's illness consists of the problems of malnutrition and withdrawal which result from prolonged inebriety. In about one-third of all alcoholics these become diagnosable mental or physical disease entities.

Dealing with the Alcoholic Emergency

In approaching the alcoholic emergency, it is essential to distinguish three treatment stages, each with its own objective. Treatment focuses successively on each of the three levels of the illness, beginning with the third. (a) *The first goal is to get the alcoholic to a physician* who can treat the physical consequences of his prolonged excessive drinking, prevent such destructive withdrawal effects as delirium tremens, and ascertain whether the person may need psychiatric treatment. A person who has been on an extended binge may need hospitalization for a few days. Treatment of his physical problems improves an alcoholic's chances of achieving permanent sobriety.

(b) *The second goal is to help the person learn how to avoid taking the first drink, thus breaking the addictive cycle.* This involves interrupting the automatic response of reaching for alcohol to handle tensions. The person must be helped to see that *alcohol* is his first problem. It is no longer a

' solution ' for him. His only hope of survival is in learning to rely on *people* rather than on a *chemical* to cope with anxiety and loneliness. If an alcoholic has medical treatment for his physical problems, but is not motivated and helped to break the compulsive-addictive cycle, his alcoholism has not really been treated. The most effective means of breaking the cycle is participation in the fellowship of Alcoholics Anonymous. The minister should urge the problem drinker to attend A.A. regularly, while he also continues pastoral counselling. The informal group therapy of A.A. complements the benefits derived from counselling. Antabuse (a drug which provides a period of enforced sobriety by its biochemical incompatibility with alcohol) is helpful to some people who cannot break the addictive cycle by A.A. methods alone. A dynamic religious experience will also break the cycle. However, many alcoholics become agnostics or atheists in the advanced stages of their illness and are driven away if a minister approaches their problem in overtly religious terms.

(c) An alcoholic is a person for whom alcohol has become a way of life. *The third goal in any effective treatment is to help him find a new and satisfying way of life to replace his alcohol-centred orientation.* This is a long-range and essential objective involving personal growth, straightening up his inter-personal relationships, finding a place to invest himself in others, and learning to draw on the help of other people and of a ' higher Power '. ' Working the recovery programme ' of A.A.—the Twelve Steps —is the most effective way of stimulating the alcoholic's growth in these areas. The steps draw on insights that are basic to the Christian tradition,

1. We admitted we were powerless over alcohol—that our lives had become unmanageable.
2. Came to believe that a Power greater than ourselves could restore us to sanity.
3. Made a decision to turn our will and our lives over to the care of God *as we understood Him.*
4. Made a searching and fearless moral inventory of ourselves.
5. Admitted to God, to ourselves, and to another human being the exact nature of our wrongs.

6. Were entirely ready to have God remove all these defects of character.

7. Humbly asked Him to remove our shortcomings.

8. Made a list of all persons we had harmed, and became willing to make amends to them all.

9. Made direct amends to such persons whenever possible, except when to do so would injure them or others.

10. Continued to take personal inventory and when we were wrong promptly admitted it.

11. Sought through prayer and meditation to improve our conscious contact with God *as we understood Him*, praying only for knowledge of His will for us and the power to carry that out.

12. Having had a spiritual awakening as a result of these steps, we tried to carry this message to alcoholics and to practise these principles in all of our affairs.[1]

In addition to A.A., some alcoholics require counselling or psychotherapy to reduce the intensity of their anxiety. Such help is usually effective only after the person has found a way to interrupt the addictive cycle of drinking. If the minister does not have the time and training to do extended counselling, a person needing such help should be referred to a mental hygiene clinic. In helping the alcoholic move toward the third goal of treatment, the minister should seek to integrate him into the web of meaningful relationships which is the heart of a church's life. Small ' koinonia ' groups, depth Bible study and personal growth groups within the church, provide an excellent resource for helping troubled people, including recovering alcoholics. As a specialized treatment programme, A.A. provides a type of help that a church cannot, but it does not eliminate the person's need for the unique spiritual help which a vital church can give. To stay permanently sober, most alcoholics must find a meaningful spiritual life. As a centre of spiritual growth, the church has an important rôle in this area.

The Hidden Crisis

There is more hope and help for alcoholics to-day than ever before in the long, dismal history of this problem. Yet, in spite of this, the tragic truth is

[1] From the ' big book ' of A.A., entitled *Alcoholics Anonymous* (N.Y.: A.A. Publishers, 1955).

that *the majority of alcoholics still die untreated* ![1]
This is due, in large measure, to the fact that the
vast majority of alcoholics are ' hidden '—either
they do not recognize the illness in themselves, or
they have managed to conceal it from the world
outside the family. Obviously, hidden alcoholism
cannot be treated.

The parish minister is in a strategic position to
bring the hidden alcoholic and his family out of
their dark closet of fear, to find help.   In his
sermons and other public statements, he can reveal
a non-judgmental understanding based on the
scientific evidence regarding the problem. He can
acquaint his people with the danger signs of the
illness and the new hope for its treatment represented by A.A. Seldom have I mentioned A.A. in
a sermon without having at least one counselling
opportunity result. If the pastor's emotional radar
is tuned to the wavelengths of persons, he will sense
that a particular family is troubled (perhaps by
alcoholism), long before they take the initiative in
seeking help.   By calling frequently on such
pastoral counselling ' suspects ', he can make himself easily available to them psychologically, encouraging them to come out of hiding and accept
help.

Creating Openness to Help

The first crucial step in counselling with the
alcoholic, as in all counselling, is to build a strong,
accepting relationship with him. This therapeutic
relationship is the instrument of help ! By intensive, disciplined listening, the pastor seeks to
get inside his world to understand how life looks
from his perspective. If a wife (or other relative)
makes the first contact, the minister should ask,
' Does your husband feel that his drinking is a
problem ? ' If possible, a session should be
arranged with the husband, to discover first-hand,
how he sees the situation. We can help people only
with problems which *they* regard as problems and
with which they desire our help. Many alcoholics

[1] Alcoholism, if untreated, reduces life expectancy by
twelve years.

make half-hearted contacts with ministers and doctors, before they are really open to help, *i.e.*, before the pain which they know will result from continuing to drink outweighs the fear of being without the anaesthetic effects of alcohol.

The minister should attempt to motivate the resistant alcoholic to face his problem and accept help. If he has been nagged or dragged to see the minister, it is essential to ' get on his side of the table ' by respecting and accepting his resentful feelings and his right not to accept help. If rapport is established with him, his drinking may be discussed. The danger signs of addiction should be mentioned explicitly, *e.g.*, drinking more than one intends, increased dependence on alcohol in stress situations, drinking alone, drinking in the morning, experiencing ' blackouts ' (temporary amnesia) while drinking, letting drinking interfere with one's marriage or job. The 'valley chart' (see diagram) is a valuable tool in counselling because it summarizes both the progression of typical symptoms and the steps which are usually involved in recovery. It is important to stress the physical aspect of alcoholism, likening it to diabetes and thus stressing the reality of the illness and the necessity of obtaining treatment. Constructive *confrontation*—' speaking the truth in love '—may be effective with the resistant alcoholic, if the minister has a strong relationship with him. This involves confronting the person with reality—the fact that his body seems to have burned out its ability to handle the chemical which he has employed to cope with stress, and, in the light of this, what is involved in learning to live constructively.

The Minister's Rôle

In motivating the alcoholic to accept the help of a physician and A.A., the minister often can use his relationship as a bridge to such resources. If a person shows any receptivity to the idea that he may have an alcohol problem, every effort should be made to provide him with an introduction to A.A. The pastor needs to know several stable A.A.

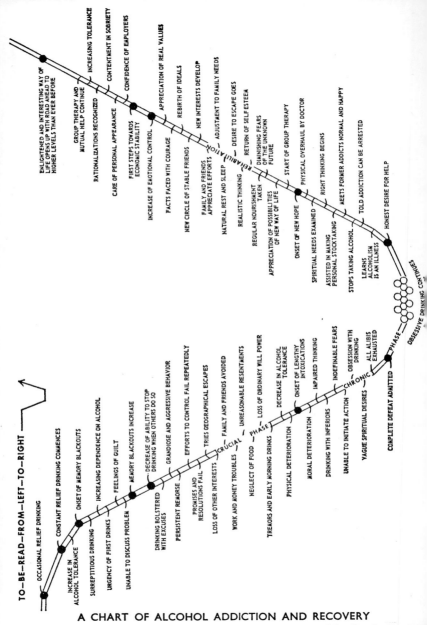

A CHART OF ALCOHOL ADDICTION AND RECOVERY

(Reprinted from The British Journal of Addiction, Vol. 54, No. 2 by kind permission of the editor, Dr. Max Glatt

members upon whom he can call for assistance. He is fortunate if such persons are also members of his church. The minister's function is to introduce the alcoholic to an A.A. member who will take him to A.A. meetings and help him identify with that fellowship. Ministers who have made little or no use of A.A. discover that their effectiveness in helping alcoholics doubles when they begin to use it as their most valuable ally in this problem.

If an alcoholic does not achieve sobriety through A.A.'s programme, the minister should help him find alternative or supplemental forms of treatment such as Antabuse and group psychotherapy. For the person who is staying sober in A.A., the clergyman can be of help by maintaining a supportive interest and by being available to counsel with him, should this be desired. The long-range rôle of the minister is the same as for any other person—to help him achieve maximum growth in his horizontal (person to person) and vertical (person to God) relationships. Counselling and personal growth groups may be highly beneficial in this process, by helping to remove the inner blocks to deeper relationships. As a specialist in spiritual growth, the minister has a unique contribution to make in helping alcoholics and their families.

The Family Illness

Alcoholism is a family illness in two senses: (a) It often results, in part, from interpersonal problems in the family, and (b) the whole family becomes disturbed and in need of pastoral help, as a consequence of the problem. Around nearly every alcoholic there is a ' circle of tragedy ' composed of the persons whose lives are most traumatically affected. The minister has an opportunity to help the wife and children, both before and after the alcoholic becomes accessible to help.

More frequently than not, the alcoholic is unready for help at the time his wife first seeks pastoral aid. In such cases, the minister can begin almost immediately to help her protect and strengthen the non-alcoholic part of the family. The pastor may need to direct the wife to the community agency where she can get financial assistance or therapy for an emotionally disturbed child. He should remind the wife who faces cruelty that no one really has to put up with such behaviour. But if there is no danger to life and limb, it is wise to encourage a wife to postpone a decision about leaving her husband until she has acquired a broader perspective on her situation, through counselling.

Beyond this, the minister can help the wife in the following ways : (1) *Encourage her to become acquainted with current knowledge about alcoholism.*[1] She needs this to cope constructively with her situation. (2) *Urge her to attend the nearest Al-Anon Family Group regularly.*[2] Al-Anon is composed of non-alcoholic relatives of alcoholics and is patterned on A.A. (If an Al-Anon group is not available, she should attend A.A.). Al-Anon attendance should continue along with pastoral counselling. Her relations with the Al-Anon group will give her massive emotional support by persons who have ' lived in the same rat-race '. They will bring her out of her lonely shell and help her handle her own problems constructively, by using the A.A. steps.

(3) *The minister should help the wife ' release ' the alcoholic who refuses to face his problem.* ' Release ', in this usage, is an Al-Anon term. It involves letting go emotionally of her obsessive struggle to ' keep him sober ' and accepting the futility of most of the things she has been doing in her vain attempts to find the (non-existent) magic key to his sobriety. Because she loves him, she must relinquish her attempt to control him. ' Getting out of the driver's seat ' takes a crushing load off the wife and interrupts much of the neurotic interaction in the marriage. Release also entails giving up any attempt to protect him from the painful consequences of his drinking by covering up for him, paying his bills, making excuses for

[1] I often loan the wife the A.A. book or the Al-Anon book, *Living with an Alcoholic* (N.Y.: Al-Anon Family Group Headquarters, 1960).

[2] The address can be obtained by contacting any A.A. group.

him, etc. He may need to suffer these consequences in order to become open to help. Protecting him from them is a form of ' cruel kindness ' which may delay his recovery.

(4) *The wife should be helped to develop the most satisfying life possible, whether or not the alcoholic stops drinking.* To do this, the wife must give up her fallacious assumption that the future happiness of the family depends entirely on his sobriety. By releasing the alcoholic emotionally and developing their own God-given potentialities for living, the family is protected from much of the alcoholic's destructiveness. In the long run, this course will also be best for the alcoholic, since it may precipitate a crisis in his life which will open him to help.

(5) *The minister should encourage mature lay people in his church to keep the family surrounded by love and concern.* This is important to both the wife and the children in that it will help them resist the dangerous tendency to isolate themselves because of embarrassment, at the very time they most need warm, supportive relationships. If the minister has selected and trained a ' pastoral care team ' of laymen to work alongside him, they can be of significant help to the alcoholic's family. In this way, a church can move toward becoming a healing-redemptive community in which ministering is a function of the whole fellowship.

Preparation for Helping the Alcoholic

Head-understanding of alcoholism—knowledge of the objective facts—though important, is not adequate preparation for maximum effectiveness with alcoholics and their families. If God's love is to be transmitted through counselling relationships, *heart-understanding* of the flesh-and-blood alcoholic is essential. The alcoholic is hypersensitive to even hidden attitudes of rejection, judgment, or condescension. He responds by returning to the oblivion of alcohol. In the final analysis, how one *feels* about the alcoholic, will determine one's effectiveness in helping him.

Heart-understanding of alcoholics is enhanced most rapidly by first-hand contacts with recovered alcoholics. Attendance, by the clergyman, at several open meetings of A.A. and Al-Anon is an essential preparation for counselling alcoholics and their families. In addition to being our best referral resource for alcoholics, A.A. is one of the most refreshing spiritual movements of our century. Many clergymen have likened it to the first-century church and have seen it as ' a modern chapter in the Book of Acts '. Reading and reflecting on the various A.A.[1] and Al-Anon books, can also increase one's heart-understanding.

Clergymen and church members often have ' passed by on the other side ' when alcoholics were involved. This has been due in part to the prevailing feeling of hopelessness regarding the problem. Such a feeling is no longer justified by the facts. If we are to be true to Him whose mission was the ' release of the captives ', we have an inescapable responsibility to help bring freedom to the alcoholic and his family.

[1] Every clergyman should own a copy of the ' big book ' of A.A., *Alcoholics Anonymous* (N.Y.: A.A. Publishers, 1955) for reading and loaning.

XVI. Drug Addiction

By Dr. Norman W. Imlah,
All Saints' Hospital, Birmingham

Advice, by a psychiatrist, on how others should
deal with the various problems created by drug
addiction must be tempered at the outset by his
awareness of two important facts. First, his own
profession as a body has so far been relatively
unsuccessful in their efforts to curtail the spread
and treat the individual ; secondly, within the
psychiatric specialty there exists widely differing
views on the ways in which addicts should be
handled, and on the best means to remove the
addiction. It follows, therefore, that one can lay
down few undisputed facts of what to do and what
not to do, but must instead draw attention
to broad general features of the varying facets
of the problem, and against this background
each counsellor must formulate his personal
approach.

It is vitally important to accept one fundamental
fact, that there is a rapidly increasing world-wide
problem of abuse of addictive drugs and unless the
trend can be reversed the consequences upon the
behaviour of society will be disastrous. A delegate
to a recent world psychiatric congress said ' Man
has found a means of destroying himself '. He
was not talking about atomic weapons, but commenting on a series of reports from all parts of the
world, each presenting a picture of a rising tide of
drug abuse in South America, Japan, United States,
Britain, Africa, Europe, and Central America, and
in every case a report of failure to control the
situation. It is of vital importance to understand
the reasons underlying this pandemic disease
because it is highly contagious and, like any other
infectious disease, must be prevented if it is to be
eradicated. It is both a very old and a very new
problem and the drugs abused are both old and
new. The form of abuse varies from culture to
culture, but throughout falls into a few defined

categories. The contrast between the old problem and the new is best illustrated by the changes seen in the United States and Britain in the last decade. These two countries, with a common language and throughout this century a gradual merging of cultural patterns, had widely differing problems of addiction ten years ago. The United States had a serious incidence of drug addiction predominantly among criminal groups and under-privileged, oppressed minorities, chiefly Puerto Ricans and Negroes. Britain had a tiny problem of some two hundred registered addicts who came almost exclusively from members of the medical and nursing professions and who had, at some time of personal stress, resorted to readily available self-medication with potentially addictive drugs. In both countries these groups still exist, but to-day there is a rapidly expanding new cultural group of addicts whose social and cultural background in both countries shows remarkable similarity. Almost exclusively they are under the age of thirty, most of them under twenty-five. They come from a wide variety of social backgrounds, as many from superficially good homes as from bad. They tend to belong to the above average intelligence category, but with wide variations. The particular drug taken varies, but a great many are poly-addicts interchanging between one available addictive drug and another, with a disturbingly high proportion on the most destructive of all drugs, heroin. Many are leading itinerant, aimless existencies, having given up all pretence at following the accepted patterns of their social background. Their prophets are men like Dr. Timothy Leary, a university lecturer, himself a drug addict, and author of a book called *The Psychedelic Approach* which an American psychiatrist recently described as ' their New Testament '. The essence of the philosophy contained in this book and propagated by other drug-addicted intellectuals is that the only worthwhile experiences are those obtained under the influence of one of these drugs ; that life has no purpose and no meaning except in this state, but under this influence the addict is like the mystic in whose mental travels the meaning of life is revealed. The words of a recent popular song ' Tomorrow Never Knows ' strings together phrases from Leary's book :

Turn off your mind
Relax and float down stream, it is not dying ;
Lay down all thought ; surrender to the voices,
    it is shining
That you may see the meaning of within
    —it is being.

The influence of such ideas among the vulnerable, immature minds of adolescence has become widespread in America and Britain. Popular culture and pop idols are often the unwitting tools of its propagation. Its dissemination originates from disenchanted groups in high schools, colleges and universities, and its victims are ranging over the whole social structure of youth. A high proportion of youth who do not take drugs are tolerant and willing to accept the views of those who do. They are hardly aware of the dangers and risks to health, and they apparently have no faith strong enough to persuade them to condemn and oppose. It is here that the doctor and the priest have a common purpose, both with essential rôles, and close unity is imperative. It may be that the newly formed National Association for Drug Addiction, in its embryonic stage mainly supported by representatives from Churches and a small group of psychiatrists, will provide a focus for united action.

The urgency of the need for preventative action is indicated by the rates of increase. Although there are wide variations in total numbers of addicts the trend is the same. The present British figures may be small compared with Puerto Rico, where one in every two hundred and fifty of the total population is a heroin addict with a fourfold increase in incidence in ten years, or New York with a hundred thousand addicts of whom sixty thousand are addicted to heroin, but it requires little imagination to envisage a similar situation in Britain. Current unofficial estimates set the number of heroin addicts in Britain around two thousand, although official figures are at half this number, but even the official figures state heroin addiction in Britain is doubling every two years with the higher rate of increase in the under-twenty-one age group. If this trend continues by the end of another decade Britain too will be dealing with tens of thousands of addicts.

Recognition and admission of the problem therefore must be made. The other essential is some knowledge of the main forms of addiction to be combated. Addiction can occur to a wide variety of drugs, but only rarely in the majority. The problem to be faced centres mainly around four groups of drugs. The first is the opium-containing drugs, of which heroin is by far the most widely abused, and is the most rapidly and completely destructive of all known drugs. Addiction to opium is a very old problem and in many parts of the world is controlled through highly organized criminal rings. It used to be the final phase of years of addictive degradation, but to-day heroin can be the starting point and we can record in this country the case of a child of fifteen admitted to hospital as a heroin addict six months after introduction to the drug.

The second group are drugs containing amphetamine, the active ingredient of the colloquial ' pep-pill '. In 1965, in Britain, one hundred million of these drugs were legally prescribed for patients, yet many doctors assert that their only proper medical use is for a small number of comparatively rare disorders. Although these drugs are not as frequently or as rapidly destructive as heroin, they induce more readily uncontrolled aggression in the individual, and to those who may underestimate the effects of these drugs it is sufficient to record that of five thousand admissions of amphetamine addicts to mental hospitals in Japan in 1955, twenty-six per cent. were still in hospital ten years later.

The drug marihuana, also known as hashish or hemp, is the most widely used addictive drug, but also the least destructive. In fact, many assert that it is not a drug of addiction at all, and there has been a dangerous tendency among many who deal with the problem partially to accept this view. Yet it has all the hallmarks of other drugs of addiction and takers experience states of excitement invariably with sexual overtones, and under its influence suggestibility to try other drugs is greatly enhanced. I believe that the adoption of a permissive attitude to this form of addiction destroys any effectiveness a counsellor may exert.

The newest and last group, the psychedelic drugs, contain the greatest potential menace to mankind of all. These drugs induce illusory and hallucinatory phenomena, distorting the perceptions to produce experiences akin to those of the schizophrenic. They came into prominence when Huxley described his experiences under the influence of mescaline in *Doors of Perception*. Even Huxley could not have dreamed up the most widely used of these drugs, lysergic acid diethylamide known as L.S.D. This drug, a synthetic product, producible without great difficulty by any reasonably competent chemist, is odourless, colourless and tasteless, and is effective in very minute dosage. A small amount in the water supply could temporarily disrupt the behaviour of a large section of the population of a great city. Reactions to it are totally unpredictable. Under its influence a man has rushed at the headlamps of an approaching car in the belief that he was catching huge yellow butterflies, while others have become acutely suicidal. Its use has become widespread among the American *avant-garde*, and is spreading to similar groups in Britain. Reports from America suggest that it is the marihuana user predominantly who turns to this kind of experience.

It may be thought that so far there has been little relevant to counselling, but the effective counsellor must be totally aware of the enormity of the problem he faces and the forces that are aligned against him. The drug addict is the most knowledgeable of all sick groups of the various ramifications of his affliction, and will have little regard for the ill-informed or the naïve traveller in his jungle.

There comes, however, the problem of the individual addict or potential addict. It has become fashionable to drop the word addiction and talk of drug abuse. Among drug abusers there are those who are drug dependent and those who are habitual drug takers. The dividing line may be a blurred one and is akin to the difference between the alcoholic and the heavy drinker, but the essential determinant of the drug dependent is the existence of a physical necessity to continue the drug. In habitual drug abuse there is a psychological dependence on the drug, but when the body becomes unable to function without the drug within, the person is drug dependent and at such a stage deprivation of the drug induces symptoms of physical withdrawal, a condition which requires medical attention. The counsellor must distinguish between drug dependence and habitual drug abuse, because in the former counselling alone cannot achieve any more than it can with any physical ailment. The initial efforts of the counsellor faced with the drug dependent must be towards acceptance of medical treatment at a recognized treatment centre for withdrawal of the drug. Provided the patient is willing to co-operate this can be achieved, and under the right conditions is very much less unpleasant than most addicts believe, and reassurance on this can be given with confidence.

The habitual drug abuser should also be persuaded to attend for a psychiatric opinion, if only to exclude the possibility of some underlying causal psychiatric illness, but it is better to delay the suggestion until confidence has been gained. Reluctance to accept such advice means that one must proceed alone, but it would be prudent for the counsellor to seek psychiatric advice on the problem, if such advice is readily available. In most cases, however, the drug abuse is bound up with traits of the personality rather than underlying psychiatric disease, and the successful counsellor must first gain confidence and respect and, through these, influence. The person most likely to help the individual will ultimately be the person whose influence is greatest, and the would-be counsellor in the situation must strive to attain this position. At the same time we must have full knowledge of our own strengths and weaknesses. Among all whose work brings them into the rôle of counsellor, there should be recognition of where we are most effective. Those among us who can be a great comfort and strength to the elderly may find that we have little influence with the young, but there are many who find that the young respond to them in a way that is lacking in any other group. This is particularly relevant to the young drug addicts, who more than most of their age have little respect for the views of older generations. If approaches are not reciprocated or contact is difficult it might become necessary to use others to achieve a breakthrough. The obvious choice for this is youth and the mobilization of the youth of a club or fellowship to this end should be considered. In such circumstances the counsellor remains in the background guiding and directing, but in a situation like this it would be important to obtain detailed reports from the young helper on all contacts with the addict including details of conversations held and to direct very closely the lines to be followed by the helper. In this way many mistakes can be avoided. It is a technique often used to advantage in psychiatry by an experienced psychiatrist with trainees.

The intelligence level of the addict must be considered and the type of counselling adopted accordingly. The highly intelligent will require to be reasoned with, and will not respond unless convinced that the ideas which led to abuse of drugs are false and that there are other values and other ideas which are more important and have greater strength. The use of reason would be largely a waste of time with an addict of low intellect, and in such a case the power of suggestion is much more likely to produce results. If suggestion is going to work there must be an incentive, and while it is generally agreed that positive incentives are more effective than negative incentives the latter should not be neglected, particularly the negative incentive of fear. A healthy fear is a very necessary acquisition for survival, and the realization of this is tending to be overlooked to-day to an extent that many young people mature with under-developed or distorted fears. The recent sharp decline in smoking among doctors probably owes as much to a healthy fear of the consequences, as it does to their conscious medical knowledge. The young addict should be factually and firmly shown the consequences of continued abuse of drugs, and the more intelligent made aware of the consequences to society of the widespread effects of drug addiction.

In considering the possibility of success an assessment of the previous personality of the drug abuser is very helpful. Where drug abuse is only one of many features of antisocial activity, such as criminal record, delinquency, sexual deviations, the prospects of sustained success are low, as the difficulties are those encountered in changing any psychopathic personality. When there is a high degree of conformity in social behaviour outwith that in direct consequence of addiction, the eventual outlook is more favourable. In no case, however, is it likely to be easy.

When one comes to deal with after-care, regarded by many in this field as the real key to success or failure, it is possible to be more definite, as the counsellor's rôle becomes a more practical one. The ex-addict is a more hopeful prospect because willingness to be cured has been demonstrated. In fact, at present, the large majority of addicts relapse after drug withdrawal and this is due to three main reasons : the vulnerability of the addict, the pressures exerted by other addicts, but mainly, the poverty of after-care facilities and workers. The ex-addict emerges from the drug withdrawal phase with no friends or acquaintances as his relationships hitherto were with other addicts and it would be disastrous to return to them. So the ex-addict urgently requires new friends to support and sustain, giving courage and strength to resist the inevitable approaches and temptations from the pushers and pedlars. This will be time-consuming as contact must be frequent and probably prolonged. Moral support must be backed in most cases by material aid. Many will be from broken homes, be estranged from families or from an unhealthy environment. In such cases a place within a family of corresponding social class and intellectual level is the most satisfactory solution, but may not be easy to obtain as a great deal of prejudice is inevitable. Even greater prejudices may be encountered when work is sought. Again this should be consistent with intelligence and abilities, and ideally should provide training. The majority of young addicts in Britain to-day have not been in a job for more than a few months, and may have hardly worked at all. Few have any established skills or trades, apart from a number who are musicians. Few have any idea what it means to work for their living, and may find routines of work difficult to adjust to, tending to revert to old patterns of frequent changes of job. They will need constant encouragement to persist, and during the early phases of after-care it is essential that there is someone and somewhere they can go to easily when out of boredom, depression, anxiety, or inter-personal difficulties they are tempted to return to the former habits. Rejection when such aid is sought would be near certain to lead to impulsive resort to drugs.

In my experience most of the young addicts will deny that they believe in God, or, if they admit the possibility that there is a God, will have rejected Him. Experience with alcoholics has shown that finding and accepting God is the most certain assurance against relapse and this applies equally to the addict. No doubt this is self-evident to the theologian, but the addict will be far less amenable than the average alcoholic and, initially, far more suspicious of the motives of the counsellor from the Church. It would be presumptuous of a psychiatrist to suggest the way in which faith and belief should be approached, but if conversion can be achieved it has great bearing on what is the ultimate object of both, namely the physical and spiritual health of the afflicted. It is well recognized in the psychiatric world that addicts who acquire faith and a belief in the teachings of the Church seldom require further psychiatric help. The addict requires material help and psychiatric treatment, but these alone are not sufficient to ensure more than an uneasy adjustment. Most are searching for something that only the Church can provide, and no doubt the rising problem of addiction presents the Church with one of its greatest challenges.

The drug addict represents the extreme of a sick society and the extent of addiction must be an indication of the state of the society in which they exist. For the most part conforming society rejects or represses the existence of the addict in its midst. A German psychiatrist at the World Congress said ' The time has come for the doctor and the addict to get together '. He was referring to the widespread aversion to treating drug addiction within the medical profession, a reluctance reflecting the attitude of society as a whole. The Church cannot be like the rest of society. Apart from the Christian example in helping the sick and afflicted, the menacing spread of drug abuse continuing unchecked threatens the structure of Christian society.

Fortunately, in Britain the Church appears to be more aware of the dangers than any other section of the community. While the medical profession are approaching the problem cautiously, politicians dawdling over the necessary legislative measures, the police impotent to act against the illegal purveyors of drugs through lack of manpower, it has been, in my recent experience, predominantly representatives from the Churches who have been most militant for action, and both nationally and locally most active in making practical attempts to grapple with the problem. The individual wise counsellor can do much for the individual addict, but the total problem can only be contained and reversed by united action in which the Church should be, and appears to be, in the forefront. It is, however, only a beginning.

XVII. The Homosexual Man

BY DR. FRANK LAKE, M.B., D.P.M.,
DIRECTOR OF THE CLINICAL THEOLOGY CENTRE,
NOTTINGHAM

Definition and the Multiplicity of Types:

HOMOSEXUALITY is sexual desire directed toward, and wishing for gratification with, members of the same sex. This may be confined to fantasies of gratification, with no actual physical intimacy. The homosexual man is usually aware of the wish to give genital expression to his affection, but this may be suppressed or apparently absent. Homosexual orientation is not incompatible with heterosexual desire and fulfilment. Kinsey expressed this overlap by a rating scale from zero to six, zero being a total absence of homosexual leanings, with presumed wholehearted heterosexuality, six being exclusively homosexual. This being so, the question, who is a homosexual man, cannot have a clear-cut answer. It is a matter of degree.

There are, moreover, many extremely different personality reactions associated with homosexual propensities. These are as far apart as the effeminate ' pansified ' personality, or the man who becomes a paragon of typically womanly skills, is from the muscle-bound, body-building specialist, who seems to be a paragon of masculinity, while lacking all confidence where husbanding is concerned, feeling free only with men.

Typology in medicine is soundest when it is derived from known fundamental causes. Even if it were agreed that the causes here are all to do with the balance of painful and pleasant experiences with women and men in the course of a man's life from infancy on, the dynamic typology remains extremely complex. It leads some to infatuations with men and boys of a certain and unvarying age or type, while others find themselves in love with men of their own age, so that theoretically they could grow old together, as the former kind cannot do.

The crux in counselling lies with the exclusively homosexual men. Kinsey rated them at 4 per cent. of the adult male population, which, in the United States, adds up to three million men. For such, homosexual activity feels as ' natural ' as the heterosexual man's love for and intercourse with a woman. Of course, moral and social disapproval superimposes a powerful verdict of ' unnatural ' upon this ' natural ' feeling, so that the initial spontaneity is overcast.

The Stereotyping that bedevils Counselling:

The time to start giving first aid to a homosexual person is not at some future date when we may be consulted by a man suffering in one of the many crises associated with the homosexual condition. The ability to help then depends largely on the extent to which we have been able already to shake ourselves free of the many misconceptions and prejudices which tend to have imposed themselves upon us. These come from within our own personalities and from many external pressures of public opinion, which have stereotyped all homosexual men in terms of the most delinquent members of the fraternity. This devaluation of a whole class of men by imposition of a stereotype is not only false to the findings of psychiatry and sociology, as disciplines attempting to keep contact with facts, it is a myth we unconsciously foster to keep our own homosexual elements rigorously dissociated from our self-awareness, as ' not me at any price '. But the price of our rather suspect denial and ruthless projection is the creation of a kind of open prison in the midst of an apparently free society, in which all those who can be identified with the accusation (not now, we note, ' diagnosis ') of ' homosexual ', have been, without possibility of appeal, condemned and put away behind the bars of social ostracism, imprisoned there for life. They are doomed by us to solitary confinement unless they can break out of it to make human contact with others of their own kind, which only confirms ' the righteous ' among us in our opinion that all such persons should be ostracised from birth to death. If they could not be physically strangled at birth, they should be slowly strangled to death by cutting off from them the air of social acceptance and loving relationships by which the rest of us live. The first step in first aid is to learn now to be shocked by the brutality of our own mass rejection, as ' right-handed people ', sexually, of those who suffer from psychological ' left-handedness '. We shall learn to be ashamed of the irrational and emotionally loaded opinion, that because some left-handed people commit crimes with their left hand, that all left-handed people are therefore criminals, from which it follows that all right-handed people are good.

Non-Recognition of the Problem, and its Non-Specific Effects:

Four out of five of those men whose erotic desire is toward their own sex, and averted from women, are not recognizable by others as having this homosexual deviation. Only one in five are recognizably ' pansy ', ' fairy ', ' queer ', ' gay ', a ' queen ', or otherwise effeminate. So, unless the majority disclose their particular secret propensity to the counsellor, it cannot be certainly known by observation of general behaviour. From this we conclude that the pastor will counsel many, if not most, of his homosexual parishioners without realizing that homosexuality is part of their problem.

Irving Bieber points out that ' In most cases the presenting and most pressing problems are the symptomatic derivatives of emotional isolation and intolerable loneliness '.

Not only is first aid given to those who know they have homosexual leanings but choose not to divulge their secret to the counsellor, it is given to others whose homosexuality is hidden from themselves. This is ' latent ', as contrasted with ' overt ' homosexuality. The paradox is that to a perceptive pastor, the latent homosexuality, for instance, of an organist and choirmaster may be more apparent, and in that sense more overt, than are the homosexual longings of a man who accepts them in himself, but for safety's sake chooses to conceal them. Latent homosexuality is closely associated with the paranoid personality, the touchy, officious individual who always feels persecuted and deprived of his rights. . This man may be much with men and boys, but if his homosexual pressures rise within him, he will come to the vicar, accusing, not himself, but another choir man, who, he feels sure, has dishonourable intentions toward his boys. He defends against his repressed homosexuality by denial and projection. The substitution, ' It's not me, it's him ' is an entirely unconscious one. Other men, particularly alcoholics, may project this guilty loving of a man on to their wives ; ' it's not me, it's her ', which is equally unconscious. In first aid no attempt ought to be made to bring about insight into this unconscious homosexuality. Help comes in other ways. We need only to be aware that accusations of guilty love of men can be displaced in this way, and be cautious when such accusations are made, lest the accuser of others be, in fact, the self-accused.

Clarifying some Practical Issues in Christian Counselling in the Presence of Homosexual Deviation:

It is because his congregation, as well as his parents and long-forgotten teachers are looking over his shoulder, monitoring his mind, that many a minister feels compelled to condemn the acts of homosexual love with a horror which the New Testament writers express equally, or more so, toward pride, blasphemy, rejection of little children, party spirit that splits the Body, lovelessness, and contempt of others, all of which flourish in the congregation without comment. The minister who welcomes homosexual persons in the name of Christ, unconditionally, must often reflect that a like acceptance could not be expected from his congregation. If they knew what he was doing, they would condemn him. We are therefore somewhat chary of expressing openly the attitude we propose to take, since charity can too readily be accused of laxity. But the homosexual man has a right to know, in these uncharted seas, to what port our own system of values would steer him, should he invite us on board as co-pilot. Non-directive counselling is only possible *within* a certain broad community of values which the therapist ought to make explicit, so that the patient or parishioner can work with confidence toward goals which are his own. I will try to think out what my own attitudes would be, and it is for others to judge whether they would like to work with them.

1. *Focus attention first of all on the non-specific personality problems such as depression.*

A homosexual orientation is so common at one stage or another of a boy's growth, from infancy to the end of adolescence, as to be regarded by many as a normal stage of development. Having attained heterosexual maturity as an adult, we hope that a happy marriage will seal a man's love of the woman, one woman, as the permanent way of his sexuality. But every ' nervous breakdown ', or ' unsurmountable emotional crisis ' in life tends to turn a baffled man back upon his tracks to look over the possibility that earlier ways of solving the problems of living and loving may again be valid. This is the mechanism of *regression*, and as such, it implies the return to the emotional perspectives of years gone by, of boyhood or babyhood, so that the pseudo-solutions it offers are not now valid. But it *feels* as if they are, and those who are in this morass of regression are usually too isolated from adult friends and helpers whose care and companionship could keep them up to date emotionally. With an adult friend alongside, who accepts what is going on, he will recognize that the seductive pleasures of adolescent fantasy lead to invalid wishes, socially unacceptable acts, and a loss of contact with his true present moment and its resources.

The clergyman whose personality includes homosexual leanings normally resists the temptation to act out his fantasies. Under severe general stress these fantasies may break out in acts which lead to his being charged with an offence. In every such case in which I have been asked to give a medical opinion to the court, I have had to represent this act as part of a depressive breakdown. For many years these men had attempted to face up to life squarely on as adequate a level of emotional adjustment as they could manage. But the scandalous loneliness of the single clegyman defeated their efforts. His is a totally uncared-for cure of souls. These sick men are the product of sick families, of socially sick congregations, in a spiritually sick church, with a sick organization of pastoral oversight. They had been experiencing the symptoms of depression, on and off, with varying severity, for years. It is not only depression, but the whole range of psycho-neurotic disorders, phobic, obsessional, hysterical, schizoid, or paranoid (for those who understand these terms), which may take their origin in or be touched off by an essentially homosexual dynamic conflict. Deal with these, then regression ceases to operate, and with it the temporary lapse into a homosexual phrase, or loss of control where homosexuality is a firm orientation.

2. *Aim to enhance such heterosexual leanings as he already has, and diminish the time and energy spent in homosexual fantasy and its acting out in homosexual genital, anal, or masturbatory intercourse.*

In proposing this target of reorientation to woman-centred sexual love, I must be honest about the many difficulties that stand in the way, and admit that they may prove insuperable in those who are exclusively homosexual. Much depends on the target the therapist proposes and believes to be attainable. Cappon, Bieber, and Albert Ellis are very optimistic of total reorientation and achieve it, or approximate to it, in a high proportion of cases, so long as the patients themselves ardently desire to change. Mayerson and Lief, Berkeley and Hooker are more hopeful than Freud, Havelock Ellis or West, and this is reflected in, or arises out of, their results ; probably both. Patients have a way of seeking out therapists whose hopes and values express their own. This will come out at the first interview.

3. *Accepting the fact that in many cases the homosexual choice cannot be dislodged, then, so far from devaluing it, I regard its lovingness as a powerfully good asset in the personality.*

I wrestle with the care of too many clergymen and doctors who neither love nor need either man or woman, whose loathing of emotional closeness and fear of bodies, male or female, is of great intensity, to underestimate the positive value of an incarnate love which reaches out beyond itself into the world of human beings in bodies, with faces, seeking a human response. Even though a series of infantile terrors blocked off this loving desire where women are concerned, and put all the stress as well as the joy of loving on to men, it remains a positive good. The homosexual man is opposed by dread of commitment only in one direction, the woman's, and that may be only in respect of sexual intercourse, not tenderness or companionship. Many of us prove under stress that we are opposed to intimate loving bonds with anyone at all. It is ironical that it is this man's healthy, loving part, put under too much pressure, too soon, by the impossibility of sexual commitment to a woman, that has now become regarded as a source of social sickness, solely because of its unruly sexual components.

4. *Whether I put this into words or not, I would feel that the aims of ' therapy ' would be furthered by his continued deep friendships with both men and women on all the levels of loving that are compatible with his own and his society's acknowledged patterns of loving.*

His own would inhibit genital activity with women, those of society would inhibit genital activity with men. The fact that English law does not now condemn the latter as criminal removes an anomaly and an injustice, since lesbian love has never been ' criminal ', though it does as much or more damage to family life, and adultery is not regarded as ' criminal ', though it does far more harm to society and its members. What is now the status in Christian counselling of these three activities, none of which is to be regarded as ' criminal ' ? At what point do any or all of them become sinful ?

I have counselled homosexual men (and married men among them) who have told me that if they so much as contemplate giving up sexual intercourse with ' the man friend ', all capacity to go on ' loving ' or tolerating their wives, if any, or to go on ' believing ' in ' God ' disappears in an abyss of hatred and wretchedness in which all hell is let loose within them. This is exactly what heterosexual men and women say when they contemplate giving up the precious object of their middle-aged infatuation. To stand by the promises of a marriage, or to stop because one's ' love ' is a factor in breaking up an existing marriage, arouses dread and disbelief in ' God '. Control is said to be impossible.

I may be mistaken, but I detect in all such cases a hidden falsity. They know that it is love of a kind that drives them. The question is, is it appropriate to the adult or to the child ? Is it mature or regressed ? Is it the product of free adult choice, or is it in fact dominated by an infantile separation panic from which it is in compulsive flight. Are most of its ' reasons ' therefore rationalizations ? I tend to believe that they are. Certainly, in those who have taken the hard way, in what they believed to be obedience to Christ, the twin aspects of dread, of separation from the new adorable image, and of commitment to a ' loveless ' relationship with an intention to love on, have been experienced with more or less intensity. They have, so it seems, to themselves and to me, been sustained in this incomparably difficult course of action by the One who invited them to it. Christ is no stranger to those final demands of anxiety which bestride all the problems of proper ' distancing ' in human relations. He is there, when the beloved is too far away, and the unloving too close. Separated from the one, and committed to the other, we groan in spirit. The Spirit of Holiness by whom all relationships are restored to, and maintained in their proper order of ultimate precedence, not of urgent persistence, groans within them in their obedience to this bilateral requirement. Golgotha, with its black dereliction, indicates Christ's passage through the one, as Gethsemane, with its bloody sweat and the cup of commitment, assures us of His conduct through the other. It is in relation to these awesome divine resources that ' sin ' is posited as a real possibility, not in contravention to the text-book requirements of ecclesiastical casuists. The potential sin is all the more real for that.

5. *The ' god ' of the religious regards sexuality of both sorts as so tainted with evil as to be itself sinful.*

We must set about correcting this false image. The equation, $sex = sin$, is terrible enough in its ruinous effects on those who can marry, but it is more terrible in the burden of guilt it brings upon the mind and heart of the homosexual man. The psychodynamic origins of homosexuality in both its components, of schizoid withdrawal from sexuality with women and hysterical clinging toward men, are so early in their onset, even in the birth process, according to the evidence I have, and in the first year of life, that all the ' badness ' of the mother-baby relationship is interpreted by the baby as ' my own, unaccountable, non-conditional, and inalienable badness '. No suffering or evil in babyhood is attributed to the mother alone. The innocent baby interprets the ' badness ' as personal $badness = guilt$. This is not moral guilt that could be ' atoned for ', by repentance or reparation. It sticks as a feeling in spite of all ' forgiveness '. Much of the counsellor's effort can usefully go into interpreting and removing these neurotic guilt feelings, since homosexuality as a particular sexual orientation is never chosen by anyone ; it is chosen for them by particular combinations of factors, genetic and constitutional (relatively unimportant), familial, parental and social (very important) over which there could be no control or choice.

Left-handed children have been made to feel guilty by teachers. Homosexual persons have been made to feel guilty by clergymen. The injustice in both cases is of the same order. To use the left hand, or the homosexual urge in ways which demonstrably injure others attracts an ethical judgment and condemnation which must stand in the courts. The death of Christ establishes this law in its exigent demand, and then meets that demand on our behalf. Similarly, as we have seen, His Cross also reconciles the afflicted to the polymorphic terrors of the caverns within them. Counselling homosexual men is a function of this *many-sided* reconciling and forgiving, mediated in a personal relationship, of unconditional acceptance, authorized and effected by Christ in us.

6. *This caring of ours need not cease even if the priest, minister, or doctor is asked to share the burden of knowing about illicit liaisons, past or present.*

The primarily religious parson, dominated by congregational and public opinion, and by ' god ', small ' g ' images of a depressive kind (' works before welcome ', ' penance before pardon ', try harder and then ' god ' will be pleased) cleanses himself from the defiling contact of one who has ' sunk so low ', by using words that create distance, judgment, and alienation.

There are times when a cynical and entirely self-indulgent attitude appals us, as when a man tells you ' under the seal ' of the number of boys in the school where he teaches whom he has had in bed with him. You are tempted to explode, and expostulate with him furiously. But the puzzle is, why did he come to tell you about it. Working out this problem, and the next moves that may bring him to his senses, requires all our energy, and our wrath works no righteousness. But to give him reasons why you believe his course of action to be wrong, and open up to him the resources of Christ for putting a final stop to it, is in my view quite necessary. It does not lose the man, and it may loosen the hold upon him of the deluded explanations by which he justifies this criminal self-indulgence. We do not add to his self-contempt by ours. Christ's care in us continues along with his judgment.

Other situations are more ambiguous. The decision of a homosexual priest to team up in a clergy house with another of his ilk, or in later life with a man in a near-by parish, may be, in many ways, the creative experience that he claims it is. What is my reaction to their determination to ' go steady ' ? Judged purely on grounds of personality development, I regret this ' marriage tie ' because

(a) It usually closes the door to further maturation in the direction of woman and the home. In answer to this it may be said with justice, ' what if that is quite impossible ? '

(b) Its close and intimate à deux closeness fosters regression with its aftermath of jealousy, envy, possessiveness, tantrums, scenes, and emotional upsets, if either wishes to have an additional close friend, apart from the other.

(c) Its intensity and privacy foster the impulse to anal intercourse or mutual masturbation and weaken the inhibitions against them. It may be answered that fine homosexual friendships have existed for years without regression or fornication.

(d) The over-intensity tends to produce a claustrophobic panic of commitment in the one, and perhaps an agoraphobic separation anxiety in the other. The first is then too often driven into homosexual promiscuity, which most homosexual men view with distaste, and the second may be pitched into a depression and/or hysterical paralysis of the personality.

(e) These pseudo-marriages tend to separate the participants off from the rest of the community more than natural marriage does—though I don't doubt that some are more open to others than many close marriages dominated by mechanisms of possessiveness, suspicion, or withdrawal in one of the partners.

7. *I trust that the net effect of my counselling will be to enable changes to take place in depth in the*

homosexual man, deeper than the areas which could be controlled by the exercise of his will.

The assumption of much pastoral advice is that men have only to exert sufficient will-power in the direction of the desired change for it to take place. Where homosexual inversion dominates a man's sexual dynamisms, the value of effort in effecting change is very limited. It may well be that the bondage of the will is paradoxical, so that the effort to love a woman, or to marry, simply arouses greater dread.

A man may suitably resolve not to delect upon his too readily available homosexual fantasies, to spend less time in the mental picture galleries where the invitations to inverted love are portrayed. He may even submit himself to psychological conditioning processes which will facilitate the development of such heterosexual possibilities as lie within him. But effort alone will not dissolve his unconscious dread of the woman, nor make the anticipations of sexual union with her delightful. Even in therapy dependent upon behavioural conditioning, he has to consent to be acted upon. To the extent that a Kinsey rating would indicate a larger heterosexual element, the part played by personal determination reinforced by conditioning therapy, will be an important one. To the extent that, humanly speaking, he is attempting a journey that can only be made by crossing his private hell, I would look to the resources implicit in his faith in Christ.

Conclusion : These considerations are some that seem to be important in a brief first-aid treatment of the subject. If it prompts someone to ask for first aid for his own anxieties at understanding so little of this increasingly spoken-about deviation, I would recommend an excellent recent book by H. Kimball-Jones, *Toward a Christian Understanding of the Homosexual* (S.C.M., 1967 ; 12s. 6d.). It has a very adequate bibliography. From this list I would draw particular attention to Dr. Daniel Cappon's book. It arises out of great experience. His therapeutic successes are an admirable pointer to possible ways forward. He would like to see the clergy trained to do a similar work. My own book, *Clinical Theology*, has a sixty-two-page chapter, based on the experience of about fifty men in therapy, fifteen of them in depth analysis, which laid bare some possible causal factors which have not yet been widely recognized.

To my readers who have more than an academic, more even than a pastoral interest in this subject, but rather a personal one, I trust I have given some help and no offence.

Editor's Note : Dr. Frank Lake in an accompanying letter insists that only one in a thousand among homosexuals requiring help can obtain full therapeutic treatment from a psychiatrist. In most cases, therefore, the help a minister or pastoral counsellor must give will not be ' first aid ', but rather the total help available to the man in need. In this situation the word ' first aid ' in the title is unreal and misleading.

XVIII. The Church and the Immigrant

By T. Geoffrey Ayre, M.W.I.,
Welfare Liaison Officer, Commonweath
Welfare Council of the West Midlands

As the spiritual centre of the community in which it is placed, the Church, like many other institutions, is finding itself involved in changes which are consequent upon the movement of population within the country itself and the impact of immigration from the Commonwealth. Many ministers are conscious, in moving into the industrial areas of our towns and cities, that new ideas, new problems, new challenges are facing them as a result of the large numbers of coloured workers living and working in the area. Other ministers are conscious of a gradual change in the constitution of their ' parish ', as old-established members of the church move away to the newer housing estates and their houses become occupied by migrant families from the Commonwealth with new and sometimes different ways of living and worshipping.

The presence of these people in our midst cannot be ignored and the need to come to terms with this new situation is a necessity for a live and virile Church. A knowledge of these new parishioners and an understanding of their special needs lead us to consider in what ways we may have a responsibility towards them. Consideration of this leads inevitably to the question as to whether the Church can minister to the needs of the newcomers without querying many things which are generally accepted and also, perhaps, without radically changing itself in the process.

The largest group of ' visible newcomers ' are those who are, in the majority, nominal members of the Church and who were at home, in many cases, active members of their denominations. These come from the islands of the West Indies, and number about five hundred thousand scattered around the country but also concentrated in the industrial areas of our larger towns and cities, where the demand for labour is greatest. The majority of West Indians come from Jamaica, the largest island in the British group, but many also come from Barbadoes, Trinidad, and the smaller islands of the Leeward and Windward group—Antigua, St. Kitts, Montserrat, Grenada, St. Lucia, Dominica, and others—and, as the average West Indian is as touchy about his homeland as the average Englishman or Welshman, it would be well to inquire tactfully a person's home territory before assuming it to be Jamaican! There is one common link between the migrants of the various islands in that they share a common ancestry, being either descendants of African slaves brought to the West Indies in the fifteenth century and after, or of mixed parentage, the end of slavery having been followed by a period when indentured labourers were brought to the islands from Spain, Portugal, India, and China.

Most of the migrants, coming as they do from an agricultural country, were small farmers, farming land which was either granted to or bought by their forbears on the abolition of slavery. Such light industries as are being developed are in the towns, such as Kingston, Jamaica, and while the government is encouraging the development of new plant and industries, nevertheless the economy is still struggling against very high unemployment and a high birth-rate, providing a clear reason for the necessity of many families to emigrate.

The word ' family ' has a much wider meaning in the West Indies than it does in this country, where it normally refers to husband, wife, and children. It is usual to regard uncles, aunts, cousins, and grandparents as well as grandchildren as ' family ' in the narrow sense of the word and it is usual for such a wider family to live clustered around a common yard. In such a household, tasks are shared out, and children are never without some one to look after them and to help in difficulties. Some of the customs stem from the days of slavery and among them the practice of ' common-law ' marriage among those who have not achieved the middle-class status to whom a church wedding would be a social occasion. The word illegitimacy does not exist in the West Indies and it is quite usual for a girl to have one or two children before considering the possibility of marriage. Indeed, it is not unknown for a minister to be asked to perform a dual ceremony, that of a marrying a couple and baptizing their children at the same time !

Many people criticize the practice of some West Indians in keeping the curtains in their houses drawn in the daytime and in not regularly cleaning their windows, but one must remember that in a country where the sun is much hotter than we usually experience here, curtains are used to keep the sun out! The fact that glass is not normally used in windows for the same reason means that it is often some time before the need for cleaning is realized. It is very easy to misunderstand the reasons for doing—or in some cases, not doing—something which concerns local customs and this illustration is intended to show the need for tact and for a knowledge of why people differ in certain practices—it would be quite untrue to assume, as sometimes is done, that a house which shows lack of attention to windows is dirty inside; indeed the standard of cleanliness in West Indian homes is exemplary.

The West Indian has an intense love of children and whatever may happen to the parents of a child, that child will usually be well cared for, if necessary by either relatives or strangers. The respect which is shown to elderly parents or grandparents is also a feature of West Indian family life and it is usual for families in this country to contribute regular amounts for the maintenance of their older relatives at home.

To most West Indians the local minister is the centre, not only of the spiritual life but of the local community, and it is quite usual to bring to him many problems of everyday life, even the most elementary, and his approval will be sought before taking action of even the simplest nature. He will be asked to visit a house just purchased or rented as soon as the key is received, in order that he may bless the dwelling before the family will set foot inside their new home and he may well be asked to perform this duty immediately on request, in spite of other commitments he may have !

The average West Indian has an unsophisticated view of Christianity and to many the ' brighter ' type of service familiar in some churches twenty years ago would hold more appeal. Many West Indians express the view that our churches are old, large, cold and the services depressingly dull. Many come to this country asserting that not only is Britain the centre of the Commonwealth and the Mother country but that Britain is the centre of the Christian faith. They experience a sense of shock when they realize how empty some of our churches are, how we are prepared to work on Sundays (providing we get ' time and a half ') and that working on Good Friday is accepted without question by the majority of people. This feeling of disappointment has led some to the Pentecostal sects such as the Jamaican Church of God which, although narrow and to some extent separatist, nevertheless provides both a brighter service and— more important in a minority group—a sense of ' belonging '.

If we consider the implications of the migration of a family from, say, the agricultural countryside of St. Kitts to the urban industrial district of Moss Side in Manchester or Aston in Birmingham, it will be appreciated that in the transference of such a family group there must be special problems of adjustment involved in settlement into such a new environment. The factory worker, his wife, and their children will each have their own problems of adjustment.

The man when he arrives will have two immediate problems, that of accommodation and of employment. He will find that accommodation is only available in certain districts and in houses which accommodate other immigrants. He could have a long search before finding a vacant room and this may be poor in standard and high in rent. His attempts to obtain employment are likely to meet

with the discouraging ' We don't take coloured '.
When he obtains a job he must then begin to try
to understand the complexities of the factory acts,
trade union rules, national insurance, income tax,
the dispatch of money to his home, and also to
cope with British weather, British reserve, British
cooking, and British factory humour—and often
discrimination.   He may also be paying back
money borrowed on his fare.   When all this is
completed and he can save money towards his
wife's fare, she will be asked to join him, leaving
the children in the care of their grandmother.
Again, the problem of adjustment is considerable.
A wife who is not easily adaptable to such changed
circumstances may soon show signs of mental
strain.   She has all the problems attendant upon
living in a single room where all one's personal
belongings have to be kept, visitors entertained,
and the family life carried on.   She must cope with
such unfamiliar matters as getting her husband
off to work at the factory early in the morning, of
sharing a kitchen and cooking stoves with other
housewives and of sharing the communal responsibilities of a multi-occupied house, of shopping
in unfamiliar shops, butchers with unusual cuts of
meat, different vegetables, the problem of choosing
clothes to suit a variable climate such as ours and
having to face shopkeepers and other shoppers
who show their dislike of coloured people openly.
If children arrive, then there is the clinic and the
hospital to cope with.

When the children at home are finally sent for,
problems of adjustment face both parent and
child.   On arrival they must conform to com-
pulsory schooling.   This means that children who
have had an interrupted schooling have to submit
to discipline after a period of ' freedom ' and
' independence ' ; they may find English schools
boring and are often restless and unruly and often
tend to idealize their home country which they
describe as ' easy ' and ' nice '.   The parents find
the children difficult to control and react either
with Victorian repressiveness or give up trying to

impose discipline. Sometimes the parents are over-ambitious for their children and the feeling that they are unable to satisfy this ambition creates feelings of guilt and frustration. In the older children there is the conflict of generations which also afflicts British children, together with the problems which surround parents who may have ambivalent attitudes towards migration and tend to wish they were back at home. This inevitably affects the children who take a long time to settle.

Many migrants are preoccupied with such problems as housing, employment, etc., and in their efforts to meet their basic priorities they pay less attention to those problems which seem to them to be of lesser importance. For instance, many migrants cannot understand why it is regarded as so important to keep medical appointments or make proper arrangements for the care of their children between the time they leave school and the time the parents arrive home from work. Many of these matters lie outside their frames of reference and they regard such matters as of much less importance than the need to work to pay high rents, to pay off debts and so on, and they are mystified by the attitude of health visitors, social workers, etc., on these matters.

It will be seen that in many cases pastoral care involves a knowledge of the background of the person seeking help, as well as skill in counselling.

So far, we have been considering those who may be ' potential church members ' ; but now we may ask ourselves if those who have come to live among us who belong to the ' non-Christian ' faiths have any claim on our thoughts and time. If we remember the words in Mt 25, ' I was a stranger and ye took me in ', and we believe that we are the instruments through which God's love pours into the world and that the Church stands at the centre of the community, then it would seem a Christian responsibility to go out to those who may be in need of pastoral care, whoever they are.

The two major groups who come into the category are the Pakistanis from both East and West

Pakistan and Sikhs from the Punjab part of India. There are also Hindus and Moslems from the Bombay province.

Both East and West Pakistanis are followers of Mohammed and number about one hundred thousand in this country. They come from two rather remote districts in the foothills of the Himalayas, Mirpur in West Pakistan and from the district of Sylhet in East Pakistan (over one thousand miles away). There is almost no industry and the economy is poor. Both people have a tradition of sending their younger sons overseas to work and help the family at home.

Islam, more than any other religion, lays down detailed requirements of a code of conduct for behaviour in day-to-day life. This is why a Bulgarian Moslem living in Bulgaria is more likely to live like a Pakistani Moslem than like a Bulgarian Christian Orthodox living next door. The word ' Islam ' means submission (to the Will of God). A Moslem must live his private life according to the principles laid down by God in the Koran. The God of Islam is, basically, the God of Judaism and Christianity. Apart from believing that there is but one God and that Mohammed is His messenger, there are four fundamentals— saying one's prayers ; fasting for one month in the year ; charity, i.e., giving away $2\frac{1}{2}$ per cent. of one's income and a visit to Mecca if possible. The Koran lays great stress on family responsibility (' Do good to your parents ') ; and there are clear regulations about inheritance. Although men and women are regarded as equal, in Moslem law the man is acknowledged as the one who carries the main responsibility. A Moslem woman is not supposed to appear or behave in public in a manner which is immodest or unbecoming. Legally women have the same rights as men and the voting age is twenty-one. If a Moslem dies, his property is divided between his children, his daughters getting one-third and the sons two-thirds. Family members are expected to be loyal to their family. This makes the average Moslem child well behaved but quiet. Moslems are forbidden to eat pig meat or to consume alcohol. Islam strongly prohibits any distinction of colour or creed. The sanctity of marriage is upheld with the greatest of reverence. The family is very strict about sexual misadventures and one never hears of a Pakistani prostitute and hardly ever of a case of an unmarried mother and in general the Moslem family lives a stable life.

The majority of Sikhs come from a region in Northern India known as Jullunder. They are the most visible of the Asians, the wearing of the turban being one of the distinctive signs of a Sikh. The sect arose in the fifteenth century and formed a bridge between the Moslems and Hindu beliefs. Fundamentally, the Sikhs are the followers of the ten teachers or Gurus beginning with Nanak and ending with Gobind Singh. They are believers in one God, in the abolition of caste and in the equality of women. The Sikh accepts the five ' K 's—the uncut hair and beard, the wearing of a hair comb, of a sword, of an iron bangle on the wrist, and of under-trunks. The Sikh religion was in its inception an attempt to find the best in both Hinduism and Mohammedism and to offer a third way, by means of a quietistic attitude, a freer social life, and a pure ethical code and a single-hearted devotion to the one true God. Their holy book, the Granth Sahib, is read in its entirety on special occasions.

The Sikhs, like all Indians, have established their extended family system here and all members of the family are closely bound together and a close association with the family left behind in India is maintained. The men are the acknowledged head of the household but the women hold the responsibility in the kitchen. It is usual to address the women through the men except with educated families. Marriages are still arranged between families although there is now some compromise among the liberal minded and educated families. Most families are vegetarians and in any case do not eat beef. It is not usual, and among traditional families not considered decent, for an Indian woman to go to work except perhaps for such professions as nursing or teaching, but this is now breaking down and a small number of women are now working in factories. Women do not go out visiting alone except among relatives or close friends. There are many Sikhs who have shaved their hair and beards since these features have been found to create difficulty in obtaining work in this country.

The three groups considered here are inevitably bringing about changes in our patterns of living : many people now eat at Indian and Chinese restaurants, families eat curries at home and the sari is regarded as fashionable evening wear in London.

What is our responsibility in this changing situation? We face a two-fold challenge. Here are large numbers of people, active or nominal Christians, who are living among us. Many are unhappy, frustrated, lacking a sense of ' belonging ', and in need of pastoral care. The churches have in the past largely neglected them, being content to say, ' The doors are open if you wish to enter '. Moreover we need to learn how to bring into the centre of church activities those who have been active in the past in the service of the church, to give them more than the job of pouring out tea, to draw them into the choir, appoint them as sidesmen, as readers, as lay preachers, and on the management committee. These things are only possible when the church is an outward-looking church which is in a real sense a ' family ' instead of an inward-looking institution. It involves each member of the congregation, young and old.

Again, are we not in danger of spiritual pride if we say, ' This is our way ; you must change your beliefs and ideas and accept our way ' ? Our churches and congregations are both meeting a new situation which requires a reappraisal of our Christian responsibility. A humble seeking after a greater knowledge of the ideas, beliefs, and practices of those who have come to live among us and of God's rôle for them in the community could lead us, through the reappraisal of our own beliefs and of the state of our church life and organization to a deeper spiritual life both as individuals and as a church.

We are not alone in considering this new challenge to our faith but are sharing it with our Christian brethren in other countries, particularly on the Continent where much larger numbers of migrants present the Church with the need to face a challenging situation.

The excitement and refreshment of spirit which comes from the absorption of new ideas, and from the meeting of new challenges and new demands is something for which we should be humbly thankful.

XIX. Uprooted People

By the Reverend Canon N. S. Power, M.A.,
Ladywood, Birmingham

The two old ladies had lived side by side, in small
back-street houses, for nearly eighty years. The
two families had always been friends, but now both
old ladies are widows ; their children have married
and moved away. In their last years, the old
ladies have been everything to each other. They
visited each other every day ; they cared for each
other in illness ; they enjoyed modest pleasures
together—a shopping expedition, a visit to a
cinema or a church outing.

When redevelopment came and both little houses
were demolished, the old ladies were given beautiful
new flats—one, miles away, the other, in the same
parish but at the top of a sixteen-storey block of
flats. Both are in danger of nervous breakdown ;
both are desperately unhappy.

George was a widower ; his wife died of cancer
some years ago and he was house-bound by a
disease of the lungs. However, George was not
unhappy. He loved to sit in his little garden,
cared for by students who came to help in our
parish by doing acts of service. He had a home-
help and the Queen's Nurse visited him. Church
members visited him, got up his coal, shopped for
him and gave him many hours of friendly company.
He loved the sporting programmes on his T.V. It
was my privilege to visit George often, to talk to
him and to pray with him. His biggest problem
was at night. When he had a choking attack, as
he often did, he used to knock on the wall. His
kind neighbours, real Christians, never failed him.
They would come in at once and help him through
the attack.

At short notice, the neighbours were re-housed ;
before we had a chance to take any action, George
faced a night alone. He had a choking-attack ; he
knocked on the wall, but the house next door was
vacant and boarded up. Next morning George

was in a state of collapse. He was taken to a local hospital and soon afterwards he died.

A doctor and an undertaker have told me, unasked, that a number of old people have died as demolition approached their beloved homes. This is also my own impression. It is just part of the tragedy when a living community, with its close and delicate inter-relationships, is torn to pieces by the bull-dozers and scattered over the city.

Old people are very dependent on the community ; neighbours shop for them, visit them, nurse them. This gives purpose to the life of the good neighbour as well as help to the old person. Good neighbours, too, have to my knowledge suffered breakdown when they were moved to places where their kindness was not needed.

It is sad to see uprooted old people making fantastic journeys to shop in the remaining little shops where they are remembered. ' It's too unfriendly out there. Here, as soon as I comes into this shop, they say " 'Allo love. How's your rheumatics ? " And they ask after Gran and little Linda. But out there nobody knows and nobody cares whether you're there or not. 'Er mother knew my Gran. I'm welcome 'ere. Where I am now they don't want to know who you are. I'll come back 'ere as long as I can.'

In some new areas, the young housewife is specially vulnerable. She has been moved from the slummy, but friendly back-street area where she knew her rôle in the community, where she was surrounded by familiar landmarks, where the doctor, minister and probably some teachers were old family friends. Her children went, probably, to a local church and belonged to its organizations. But above all, ' mum ' was not too far away. The three generations were closely linked by bonds of love and mutual aid. In times of anxiety ' mum ' could be relied on as counsellor, baby-sitter, and confidante.

In the new area, the young mother can be desperately unsure of herself. The familiar landmarks are gone. The people round her are strangers ; they all seem as smart as she looks (without realizing it) to them. She feels no natural attachment to the local church or clubs or the strangers who go there. Lonely and disorientated, she is concerned with outward appearances and may become withdrawn, suspicious, and house-proud, anxious to keep up to the new standards. Worst of all, ' mum ' is far away. Sometimes she feels she has no one to turn to. She may become depressed, to the detriment of the whole family. Thus ' New Town Neurosis ' begins.

The young people are similarly affected. Dis-orientated, their lives, above all, lack challenge and purpose ; with the wide-spread abdication of responsible parenthood, especially by the father, they have no way of life, and no standards such as are given by a lively Christian faith. The only values they see are commercial values. Situations that ' give a kick ' to life have to be manufactured. This, of course, is not so true of the Grammar School children from good homes, as of the children in the lower streams of the Secondary Modern School. One answer may be the ' Com-prehensive School ', but I fear that these schools may be too big to provide what is most needed— a sense of belonging to a compact, united and caring community.

People who attack religion in schools—and often those who reply to them—always approach this question from the wrong angle. It is not so much the dogmatic teaching that may be valuable as the experience of belonging to a Christian community. Too many young people are growing up in isolation from any real sense of community. Small schools, instead of being cherished, are liable to be closed. In place of a true community, making strong demands as well as strong providence, they know only a state which seems to have set itself the ideal of eliminating any sense of responsibility ; it offers too much padding and too little else.

Experiments made in connexion with the pro-blem of ' weightlessness ' in space-travel indicate the dangers of disorientation. I have heard Dr. R. A. Lambourne, consultant psychiatrist at Rubery Hospital, Birmingham, (and author of a magnificent book, ' Community, Church, and Healing ') describe in a lecture the effects of disorientation. He explained how our sense of personal identity, far from being an immutable possession to be taken for granted, is a fragile possession that we can lose. We need to retain our consciousness of identity by contact ; every casual contact helps us—even contact with the chair we sit in helps to identify us as the person sitting in the chair. In the experiments, the subject ' floats ' in a tank of water at body-temperature. All outside stimuli are removed. There are no contacts. Comfort is absolute, but the subject may become deeply distressed. First, he experiences hallucinations, then loss of identity. Finally he may become violent and ' lashes out ' in search of contact. This is disorientation. Dr. Lambourne believes this is equally true psychologically. We need contact with family, with neighbourhood, with nature, and with the ground of our being, which is God.

This, I believe, helps to explain the unprecedented rise in crime and vandalism, in violence and drug-addiction, not in a time of unusual poverty, but in a time of unparallelled affluence and vast schemes of re-housing. In this situation the Church has the answer. Instead of losing heart, the Church and her Ministers should be proclaiming the answer from the house-tops, the answer to the need of our time.

It is in the Christ who meets us at the point of our need wherever two or three are gathered in His name, in the challenge of that caring community which is His body in the world, in the service of the unfolding purpose of His Kingdom, which is God's Kingdom, in the work of the good neighbour in a world desperate to rebuild community.

This is where the Welfare State fails. In a Welfare State we *are* contributing to each other's welfare, but it is all too impersonal. Somehow the State has failed to challenge our idealism or make our contribution to the welfare of others a joy.

In the uprooting of families, it is the children

who suffer most. At a time when there is inadequate affection and care in many families, children rely to a great extent on the community—on teachers, minister, club-leader, on ' grans ' or kind neighbours.

It is only in the better families, to-day, that children are really loved, played with, taught to enjoy books and games, given the experience of a living faith or taught to pray. After fourteen years I still wait for the first father to come and watch his son play football. Often, in our clubs, we have to teach children to play the family games our parents taught *us*.

Once I met a little boy of six who could not speak. I took him to an expert who found nothing organically wrong. After two weeks, the boy was talking enough to make himself understood and I asked him why he had never spoken before. ' Well,' he replied, ' no one ever spoke to me.' He had T.V. What more could he want ?

Let me introduce you to Richard and Joan. Richard was first brought to my notice as a ' problem child ' who attended one of our Church Schools. He had set on fire the curtains at home and thrown all the crockery he could lay hands on out of an upstairs window. He seemed docile enough, a pale, thin, and rather ragged, dirty child of some seven years. We agreed to take him to Camp for a week. At Camp, one of our lady helpers agreed to ' Mother ' him. She even let him sleep with her own little boy . . . a kindness for which there was a price to be paid ! (In fact, our work involves a constant battle with ' flies, fleas, bugs, and beetles ', and more difficult enemies ; the more we try to help ' problem children ' the more liable we and our children are to pay the penalty !) This little boy was in heaven at Camp. He not only had his first real holiday, but his new friend was always willing to let him hold her hand . . . and he asked nothing more. At Camp, I always tell the boys a story at night. It is interesting to see how quite big boys gather round for this, even trying to get as close as my own children so as to feel ' part of the family '. No child ever enjoyed the stories as much as Richard. Sitting next to me, holding his new friend's hand, I suppose he felt for the first time in his life the security of belonging to a family.

Since then I have found out a great deal about Richard and his ten-year old sister, Joan (not their real names, by the way). Their mother never had much use for them; they had frequent beatings but little other attention. She lived with a succession of men and finally cleared off with one of them, abandoning the children in an empty house. An old 'Granny' offered to take them in; within a few days she had had a stroke and now the children look after her. Joan does all the housekeeping, shopping, cleaning, and cooking after school hours. But if the Welfare Department take over it may mean separating the children, who are devoted to each other.

It is now obvious that Richard's naughtiness was simply to attract attention—a beating was better than nothing. Also he felt deprived—he knew not of what—and therefore resentful. It is easy to understand and sympathize when he is seven. When he is seventeen he will be classed as a thug unless someone shows him enough affection to undo the harm that has been done. We shall do our best. But the great danger will be when he leaves our Church School at eleven.

Meanwhile, these children are frequent visitors in our home. We seem to be able to give them a feeling of security in our affection. Joan has been Confirmed and she and Richard now often smile— a thing they never did before. It shows what can be done just by awareness of the problem—the desperate need for affection of children, uprooted or from deprived homes—and by keeping ' open-house ' for such children.

One problem is the segregation of the country into one-type areas, so that those who might be aware of the problem, and make a positive contri-bution to it (doctors, teachers, etc.) are liable to live miles away in ' respectable ' suburbs. This can only be remedied at local government level, by allowing Housing Trusts to vary the monotony of council housing. There is, happily, evidence that some Councils are alive to the problem.

I cannot exaggerate the dependence of many children on their teachers, ministers, and club-leaders for an affectionate relationship. Many children in our church day-schools call the teacher ' Mummy '. We keep open house for such children and our home is always full of them. One little girl of seven had been to five schools, owing to frequent removals. She refuses to talk or to accept any relationships. She has been ' bereaved ' too often. Unless we can break through, she is sure to become delinquent, but even if we do, may she not be moved away again ?

All this is the background of our common problem, the problem of the breakdown of community life.

Much can be done through sympathetic councillors to re-house old friends and neighbours near each other. We can gather together uprooted old people in ' Darby and Joan ' and other clubs. Here we have just started an additional experiment, a factory in our Church Hall for ' The Sheltered Employment of the Elderly '—without any loss of pension or other rights. Kind firms supply work and the governing body, at Civic level, provides the supervisor's salary.

Club life helps the young mother ; the Toddlers Club gives her some freedom and she can discuss her problem with the church members in charge. The church can provide a rota of sitters-in. A visiting team from all the local churches, including the Roman Catholic, seeks out the lonely, the old, the house-bound, and depressed, referring back special problems to the ministers. A deliberate effort can be made to seek out deprived children, to give them affection, to keep ' Open House ' for them. We take some fifty such children, and others, for a week by the sea every year. We have taken over a thousand in twenty years.

Understanding the problems gives point to counselling. As the caring community the Church can meet these different categories of people at their point of need. One reception-area church invited me to speak to a group of old people up-rooted from Ladywood, gathering them together for the purpose. This helped them to reorientate themselves in their new area. Young people have found purpose as members of visiting teams and as helpers in taking children for excursions. Girls from a Home-Office Home have done splendid work by taking out in bath-chairs cripples from a local hospital for such people.

But I believe with all my heart that the Churches must speak with one voice against the destruction of communities in re-development. It can be avoided in slum-clearance ; it has been avoided at Oldham and in West German slum-clearance schemes. The greatest service we can do is to prevent people from being uprooted in the first place.

' There is no life that is not in community and no community not lived in praise of God.'

Acknowledgment is made for permission to use extracts from *The Forgotten People*, published by Arthur James Ltd., Evesham.

XX. Community and Communication

By Dr. Brian Lake, L.R.C.P., L.R.C.S., D.C.H., D.P.M., Clinical Theology Centre, Nottingham

Society in past generations frequently dealt with those who were mentally and emotionally distressed in a painful and inhuman way. Many people nursed their crippled emotional lives without sympathy or enlightenment, although religious and social movements then, as now, helped many of those who lived an intolerably cramped existence to experience new areas of freedom and justice. In our own time the mental hospitals have been revolutionized ; local authorities, social case-work agencies, adult and juvenile courts have begun to absorb and put into effect the new insights of psychology and the social sciences. But so far no method of treating the neuroses has been found which is not time-consuming. A number of psychiatric disorders have been relieved by new electro-chemical methods, but a pill has yet to be found which transforms human personality to such an extent that it makes it possible for us to believe in the dawn of a new life of peace and harmony. Even if it were, it could certainly be guaranteed to present problems of addiction and physical side-effects !

In the last twenty years, therefore, the medical world and its allied professional helpers have been faced with the problem of finding some way of helping large numbers of people presenting disabling neuroses. A stage has arrived when society has been asked to take some part in a therapeutic programme, and to regard itself as a therapeutic community. The difficulty is that increasing enlightenment seems to have led to increasing demands for treatment, and demand greatly exceeds supply. Nor is the situation relieved by the increasing mobility of our society. The gradual disruption and fragmentation of natural groupings of friends and family has meant that many who previously were able to seek help in a reasonably stable setting now find their way to the general practitioner or casework agencies. Mental and emotional illnesses amongst the elderly are frequently precipitated by isolation from their families ; widows grieve without support ; young married couples and their parents miss the mutual support they can give to each other; children and adolescents reflect the atmosphere of insecurity which follows the general loosening of ties to old-established groups. These and many other contributory factors add to the problem of therapeutic availability.

It is in this context of group disruption, with its grievous emotional consequences for those who are still especially dependent on them, that group treatment has become a vital part of present-day therapy and research. This research has amplified our knowledge of those aspects of group life which are responsible for sustaining or damaging a proper development of personality. It shows conclusively that, and explains some of the reasons why, the groups to which we belong at our most impressionable age are of profound importance in creating moral attitudes and habits of social behaviour. In them we learn by the usual processes of training, belonging and participation, how to make contact and communicate with other people, and we carry with us throughout our lives these vital imprints of experience. In this respect the study has enlarged the scope of diagnostic and preventative measures in individual and social sickness and provided new techniques in the sphere of treatment. It underlies the assertion that society itself must become a healing community, and that no one can plead complete ignorance of the dynamic forces in group interaction which lead to health or illness. It is perhaps because no one has emerged entirely unscathed from these experiences that the community is not as therapeutic as it might be. Our parents were often concerned about the school or church we went to, and the groups to which we belonged, but the primary group for which they were responsible was sometimes structured and influenced consciously or unconsciously so that it thwarted the development of many of our valuable assets. They had their unquestioned basic assumptions and values, and some of them blurred and blunted our perceptions. We absorbed to the core of our beings their religious and cultural attitudes, and some of them deprived us of emotional needs, left dormant physical and mental skills, and repressed spiritual and creative capacities.

Now that we have a wider appreciation of these factors which play their part in moulding all our lives, and the needs of those who are in anguish because they were deprived of even the elementary constituents of personal being and well-being, the responsibility of meeting some of these needs is imperative for those to whom much or little has been given. One of the difficulties of the past has been that professional helpers have underestimated the resources of ' ordinary ' people and there are still conservative elements who resist any attempt to develop and train the therapeutic potential of the laity.

Despite attitudes such as these, and perhaps because of them, the new ideas of social and administrative psychiatry have permeated a number of mental and general hospitals. Stereotyped leadership patterns have been scrutinized for attitudes which lead to loss of initiative and institutional neuroses amongst patients and staff. Democratic concepts have been introduced, with every member of staff undergoing some analysis of previously unquestioned assumptions. Lines of communication between patients and staff which were previously blocked have been opened up, and suspicions which previously led to repressive attitudes have been clarified and relieved. Most of these improvements, in conjunction with the new electro-chemical techniques of treatment, have been brought about by courageous and patient experimentation in group and social methods. Modifications have had to be made for those who need a more individual or authoritarian approach, but improvements leading to increasing trust and responsibility between patients, staff and relatives have been sufficient to lead to the introduction of these new principles to an everwidening circle of medical institutions. A great deal more work is necessary in clarifying these problems of communication, and deeper studies are being made on group aspects of psychological development in infancy, childhood and adolescence. New insights are being used in family group sessions which enable parents to restore security and love to the children they had previously deprived. ' Small table ' techniques are used for toddlers and kindergartens. Group therapeutic techniques are used in residential units for handicapped children, delinquents, psychotic children and adults, alcoholics, the psychosexually disordered, unmarried mothers, disturbed adolescents, and in the wider range of psychoneurotic disorders. The aim is always to increase each individual's capacity for communication, without which he remains isolated, alienated and unable to open himself to others. Conflicts and fears remain hidden, problems remain unexpressed, suspicions grow deeper unless some means are devised to overcome or at least relieve these obstructions to human relationships and personal development. This is equally true for industrial, social, religious and professional organizations and national bodies as it is for the recognizably disturbed individuals in society.

It is because of this that the study and analysis of this new learning needs to be undertaken by professionals and laity, leaders and led, employers and workers. This will not only lead to a greater understanding of their different functions but to the possibility of alleviating many of the visible or subtle causes of psychological violence. The stalemate which results from hierarchical reactionary attitudes in whatever political or social system we care to think of always leads to the development of new interest in authentic scales of value, and a willingness to learn by trial. Some of the errors have led to equally repulsive violations of human freedom. The fight to raise emotional and spiritual experience is always fraught with danger and the possibility of enslavement by new techniques of force, each more subtle than the other. At this transitional point we need the safeguard of a synthesis between contemporary religious and philosophic thought, with its subjective and introverted approach, and intellectual objectivity concentrated in the realms of science. It is only when this is achieved that we can hope for an integration of love, power, and justice.

By way of introduction to group therapy, it seems easiest to discuss briefly the effect of forms of leadership within groups, and to mention different types of groups whose primary aim is to benefit the individual. It seems part of the natural order that every group has its leaders; the father or mother, schoolteacher, priest, manager or politician. J. A. C. Brown in his book *The Social Psychology of Industry* divides leaders into the following broad groups: the strict autocrat who fails to delegate authority and controls his country, parish or hospital as a one-man show— he usually has conservative and anti-feminist leanings and is decent to his men providing they ' know their place '; the benevolent autocrat practises a more refined tyranny, wanting to do people good but taking upon himself the onus of deciding what is good for them; the incompetent autocrat is domineering and erratic, frequently scapegoating others for his own failures, promoting lieutenants because he feels insecure and believing in the all-powerfulness of his wishes; the genuine democratic leader is a person who can listen, arbitrate, delegate authority all the time and provide proper communication between all levels; the pseudo-democrat wishes to emulate this sort of leader but is too insecure to make a success of it; a *laissez-faire* leader is represented as one who leaves all responsibility and most of the work to his subordinates. If he is reasonable, he acts as a sort of figurehead—ornamental without being a nuisance. Brown sees these types of leadership as operating at all levels of management, as foremen, statesmen or Churchwardens.

Therapeutic groups, therefore, frequently discuss the problems of leadership and of the effects of working under varying types of leader as far as their emotional feelings, morale and effectiveness are concerned. What sort of leadership, for example, leads to the development of individual potentialities and acceptance of responsibility ? What produces general or particular hostility, and why ? Do certain defects in the interpersonal relationships of a congregation or shop-floor, and its effective functioning as a group, stem from unsuitable ideals and patterns in leadership ? Père Congère has recently questioned the leadership of Bishops in his own Church in the following statement : ' They have a certain contact with men, but the contact is fenced round with protocol and marks of respect. In these circumstances men are careful not to say too much ; they generally encounter an artificial rather than a real situation.'

Those who want a more detailed knowledge would do well to read Foulkes and Anthony's book on *Group Psychotherapy*. They will find that a new awareness of group phenomena has developed, and a specialized terminology, with such words as ' chain ' or ' condenser ' phenomena, ' scapegoating ', ' pairing ' and ' subgrouping ' to describe certain group situations. These and many others are a means to better understanding and communication in group relationships.

The main function of these groups, however, is to assist in the process of healing, and different types of group are required to meet the particular needs of those with particular problems. Selection is of vital importance. It is because of this that patients are often received into a preliminary group and moved later to a preparatory group before joining as members of special groups. These may be ' Supportive ', ' Educative ' (talks, discussions, films, etc.), ' Work ' (building, cleaning, gardening, etc.), ' Physical ' (table-tennis, rambling, games, dancing, etc.), ' Creative ' (art, music, play readings, etc.). The group is organized around this activity. Whatever the occupation, the sense of belonging and participation in the group activity is of primary therapeutic significance, and the occupation of secondary importance. But both are clearly important in that they give each person in the group an opportunity to develop and utilize their faculties and skills with a purpose in view, and enable them to overcome their anxious egocentricity. The work or creative activity serves as a catalyst, and provides an objective subject for discussion. Soon the dynamics of participating together, decision making and group needs become the talking point. It is here especially that the value of ' good ' leadership becomes paramount in the ' formation ' of a ' good ' group. The sort of leader required is one who accepts each person and the whole group, helps to draw out potential skills, brings into the open hidden points of friction, initiates, informs, clarifies and summarizes interests, and creates a spirit of enthusiasm and group morale. With good leadership members of the group know their function and learn to work together. They discuss their aims, devise their own modes of participation, discipline and responsibility, and each member takes his place in a larger group fulfilling a significant rôle in it.

The psychotherapeutic group differs from those previously mentioned in that it relies on verbal communication as the only activity. The group is treated for the sake of its individual members and is the main healing agency. Psychotherapeutic groups can be divided into two broad categories which reflect a similar division in individual therapy. There is group analytic psychotherapy with some variations of technique, depending on the particular analytic school of the group analyst, which can be regarded as a radical approach, and group psychotherapy which contains a broad spectrum of differing techniques and suitable for more peripheral and symptomatic purposes. Classification is, however, extraordinarily complex in this field, techniques and levels of operation varying from one group to another. Both these forms of therapy require the assistance of a person trained in analytical, technical, and practical aspects of group psychodynamics. They are in fact experts in verbal and non-verbal communication within the group, and help in the process of making conscious the emotional experiences which individual members are unaware of or afraid of voicing. They study all the interactions within the group, map out like meteorologists (by recording and translating observable data) the locations of high and low emotional pressures and interpret the causes. In this way each member is helped to increase his capacity for verbal communication of previously suppressed feelings. The result is that in this atmosphere of perceptive tolerance the silent begin to talk and conversational monopolists become more subdued ; defensive attitudes begin to break down ; bottled up feelings are released ; guilt feelings alleviated ; information and life experiences exchanged. Acceptance gradually arises from within the individual as a result of better communication and a deeper understanding of the forces involved in the subjugation or distortion of particular emotions.

It is quite impossible in the space of a short article to outline even the major findings of present-day research in this field. But sufficient may have been said to show that a number of these findings can be of great value in diagnosing causes and relieving the malaise of a multitude of groups within our society. The field is an enormous one and much of the work is still in an experimental stage. The situation is in some ways analogous to the research performed by early epidermiologists in the field of infectious diseases in the last century.

The difficulty at present is the translation of these technical findings and achievements in such a way as to modify and transform the attitude and behaviour of ever-increasing circles of individuals within the community.

A prime mover in this work has been the Institute of Human Relations at The Tavistock Clinic, which has provided research facilities and courses for leaders in industry and the professions and inspired an increasing number of State and voluntary casework agencies to include this discipline in their programmes. But what of the Church's attitude to this new and yet old process of interpretation and communication ? Is there any assessment of the value, the similarities and differences between modern psycho-therapeutic methods and, for example, the rules of the Methodist Band Societies (1738), based on early apostolic practice ? The design of their small group meetings, which were held punctually every week, was for each member in order to speak ' freely and plainly the true state of our souls, with the faults we have committed in thought, word and deed, and the temptations we have felt, since our last meeting ', and that each person ' ask the rest in order, as many and as searching questions as may be concerning their state, sins and temptations '. They were in fact described by Thomas Coke as ' spiritual hospitals '. There is no doubt that Churches in the United States of America, with their advanced University and hospital programmes of pastoral psychology, use both individual methods of counselling and many modifications of modern group psychotherapeutic techniques in their numerous small group programmes. In England the response has been more cautious and conservative, but a number of organizations have made a useful start. Christian Teamwork which was established in 1957 ' to equip Churches to exercise leadership in tackling the social, industrial, pastoral, and personal problems they encountered in the course of their day-to-day lives ' has developed courses in collaboration with the Tavistock Institute, which would bring together the study of human behaviour and examination of the question of what God is doing in industry, society, and particularly human situations. The Church of England Board of Education provides courses on leadership training and small group work, with emphasis on learning, decision making, the rôle of the observer, stereotypes, etc. The Clinical Theology Association, whose aims are to promote understanding between the disciplines of psychiatry and theology in the training of clergy and other interested professions, include group dynamics and training in their widespread seminar programmes. Over three thousand clergy have undertaken this training.

These and other organizations show that Christians are prepared to equip themselves by using and modifying these new techniques in mediating the knowledge of the love of God to men and women in every field of human activity. But this is only a beginning. The Church and other organizations are all potentially capable of a wider and deeper application of these new insights. When fully applied to the problems of leadership and communication in the administration of parishes, deaneries, and dioceses, and in the pastoral care and the cure of souls, the cross-fertilization between the two disciplines of psychology and theology could well bring to the Church an authentic renewal and reformation. After all, Christianity began as an adventure in a small group movement. It is now a world-wide society of small groups with the whole Body committed to the corporate life of each individual and every group : ' Bonded and knit together by every constituent joint, the whole frame grows through the due activity of each part, and builds itself up in love '.

References and Bibliography

The Social Psychology of Industry by J. A. C. Brown ; Penguin Books.

The New Group Therapy by O. Hobart Mowrer ; Van Nostrand Insight Books.

Experience in Groups by W. R. Bion ; Tavistock.

Group Dynamics by D. Cartwright and A. Zander ; Tavistock.

Human Groups by W. R. Sprott ; Penguin Books— Pelican.

Working with Groups by Josephine Klein ; Hutchinson.

Group Psychotherapy by Foulkes and Anthony ; Penguin Books—Pelican.